C.S.A.
OUR HEROES
issippi

to
Lori Danny
Walt Grayson
11·8·10

Oh! That Reminds Me

Mississippi

More Homegrown Stories

WITH Walt Grayson

Mississippi is known for its rich soil and the bountiful crops it produces. But it is best known for its homegrown people and the rich traditions they have established and sustained over the years. Join Walt and many other Mississippians as they open their life albums and share their memories in words and photographs.

Electric Power Associations *of Mississippi*

A network of twenty-six electric cooperatives serving more than 750,000 members with affordable, reliable electric service

www.epaofms.com

It's a matter of
PERSPECTIVE
To most this is just a country road. But at electric power associations, we know it's roads like this that lead to the future. More than seventy years ago, some said our plan to bring power to rural Mississippians wouldn't work. Yet, we listened to the people and developed a network of member-owned and not-for-profit electric cooperatives.
Today, we're still listening because we know that without power, there is no growth And without growth, Mississippi's future would look pretty dim.
That's why electric power associations continue to build and plan today, so all our tomorrows can be a whole lot brighter.
Electric Power Associations . . .
. . . improving the quality of life for the 1.8 million Mississippians who receive affordable and reliable electric service in the communities we serve.

Electric Power Associations . . .

exemplify the power of working together

What does "homegrown"mean to you? Fresh, ripe tomatoes? Soul-stirring gospel music or deep-fried catfish?

"Homegrown" describes any number of Mississippi traditions—including rural electric service. If that surprises you, consider this: The state's twenty-six electric power associations are rooted in a homegrown initiative that lifted rural residents from the "dark ages" into a brighter future of social and economic progress.

Electricity was widely available in towns and cities in the early twentieth century, but rural Mississippi was still in the dark. Less than 1 percent of Mississippi's 311,683 farms had access to electric power as late as the 1930s. Household and farm chores were time-consuming, strenuous and exhausting for rural people without the benefit of electric equipment and appliances.

Hope appeared on the horizon in 1935, when President Franklin Roosevelt created the Rural Electrification Administration (REA) by executive order. The following year, Congress passed the Rural Electrification Act to make possible reliable, high-quality and affordable electric service to all rural Americans.

Mississippi quickly emerged as an early leader in the nation's rural electrification effort by passing laws for the formation of electric cooperatives, or electric power associations.

Rural electrification's impact in Mississippi was as life-changing as it was innovative. Far more than simply lighting up homes, it empowered rural residents to create unique electric cooperatives based on local needs. This, they understood, was the necessary first step toward improving their dismal quality of life.

Within five years, rural Mississippians had organized twenty-five consumer-owned electric power associations. Each was a private enterprise owned and operated by the people it served.

As new power lines began crisscrossing the countryside, a thriving market for electrical appliances followed. A 1939 REA survey indicated that 75 percent of Mississippi electric power association members had purchased a refrigerator, a water pump, a washing machine or a radio.

Farm efficiency soared as farmers took advantage of new electrical equipment—milking machines, dairy refrigeration, poultry incubators, brooders and the like—to help boost production and reduce manpower.

The expansion of rural electrification stalled when the World War II shortage of copper and other materials forced a halt to construction throughout the nation. The postwar years, however, saw a resurgence in line construction. Electric power association membership grew in number and diversity as rural electric power presented new commercial opportunities beyond city limits.

Mississippians now expect affordable electric energy to be available at any moment, regardless of where they live. Electricity is neither a luxury nor mere convenience, but a necessity for their quality of life.

In recent decades, "quality of life" has come to mean far more than the distribution of high-quality electricity. Today's electric power association members also depend on their cooperative to:

- restore electric service quickly, efficiently and safely during power outages, and help rebuild communities after natural disasters
- monitor energy-related state and federal legislation to safeguard their interests and the affordability of their electric service
- stimulate economic development by helping attract new business and industry and encouraging the expansion of existing enterprises
- prepare for tomorrow's electric power needs to enhance reliability and affordability
- serve as an authoritative source of information on energy efficiency, electrical safety and other energy-related topics.

Homegrown and home owned, electric power associations exemplify the power of Mississippians working together.

Electric Power Associations . . .

a true homegrown story of our own

The family of electric power associations is proud to present the third in a series of "Looking Around Mississippi" books with Walt Grayson. We took a unique approach to this special edition by inviting Mississippians to share their photographs and stories with you. And it has proven to be a true Mississippi book. Special thanks to the more than eleven hundred people who submitted photographs of life in our great state. We enjoyed viewing everyone's entry, and it was a difficult task to select the ones to publish.

Publishing this book reminded us that life is great in Mississippi and family traditions are cherished. I am constantly reminded that we are truly a state with a lot of homegrown stories. From Mississippi's world-renowned musicians and writers to natural beauty and tourist sites, ours is indeed a beautiful state. That's why we chose the title *Oh! That Reminds Me: More Mississippi Homegrown Stories*.

But the one thing that separates us from other states is our people. They are hardworking, strong in values and courageous in their effort to ensure Mississippi continues to be a great place to live and work. Each day they awake with a purpose, to contribute in a manner that will make a difference in the lives of others. They have not forgotten the cherished memories of the past, as you will see on the following pages, as they look to make the future even brighter.

As you look through the book, remember the many people who have dedicated their lives and invested their hard work to attain the quality of life we treasure and future generations will appreciate. One such group is the people who brought electricity to the rural areas of Mississippi. More than seventy-five years ago, they planted a seed that led to another true homegrown story: the twenty-six electric power associations who provide reliable and affordable electric service to more than 1.8 million Mississippians. Today, each of us enjoys the fruits of their labor.

This tradition continues with a dedicated workforce of more than twenty-six hundred Mississippians working tireless hours to ensure you have electric service at the lowest cost possible. These men and women are part of your community and serve in many areas. We salute them for a job well done. From our family to yours, we hope you enjoy this "homegrown" book produced by Mississippians.

Michael Callahan, CEO

HALEY BARBOUR
GOVERNOR

STATE OF MISSISSIPPI
OFFICE OF THE GOVERNOR

Dear Friends,

Governor Haley and Marsha Barbour

A good storyteller and a good story to tell are a match made in Heaven. Mississippi has a great story, and with his eye for detail, Walt Grayson tells our story extremely well.

Oh! That Reminds Me: More Mississippi Homegrown Stories is one part travel guide and one part history lesson. It's a peek into our culture and our character, and the connections that run through all Mississippians, from the Delta to the Red Clay Hills, from the birthplace of Elvis and the birthplace of America's music to the home of resilience and self-reliance. And, of course, the hospitality and heritage that course through Mississippi's cities, small towns and crossroads are among our world-renowned hallmarks.

There is so much awesome beauty throughout the state, and Walt's words and the photographs paint the picture of Mississippi and her residents. Over the years, we've had our challenges, but because of the indomitable spirit rooted deeply into generation after generation of Mississippians, we've met those challenges head-on. We've answered each call, and we've come back stronger.

As Governor of the State of Mississippi, I want to thank you for your interest in the state we love so much. If you already live here, please take the opportunity to visit other areas of the state. If you're visiting, I hope you'll consider this an invitation to come see Mississippi again and again, and experience the sites and the hospitality for yourself.

Sincerely,

Haley Barbour
Governor

Oh! That Reminds Me

Mississippi

More Homegrown Stories

WITH Walt Grayson

THE
DONNING COMPANY
PUBLISHERS

The Donning Company Publishers
184 Business Park Drive, Suite 206
Virginia Beach, VA 23462

Steve Mull, General Manager
Barbara B. Buchanan, Office Manager
Richard A. Horwege, Senior Editor
Brett Oliver, Graphic Designer
Derek Eley, Imaging Artist
Neal Hendricks, Project Research Coordinator
Tonya Hannink, Marketing Specialist
Pamela Engelhard, Marketing Advisor

Neil Hendricks, Project Director

Electric Power Associations of Mississippi
Michael Callahan, Chief Executive Officer
Ron Stewart, Senior Vice President
Debbie Stringer, Editorial Support
Mark Bridges, Graphic Support
Jay Swindle, Marketing
Linda Hutcherson, Administrative

Library of Congress Cataloging-in-Publication Data

Grayson, Walt, 1949–
Oh! that reminds me : more Mississippi homegrown stories with Walt Grayson.
p. cm.
ISBN 978-1-57864-637-1 (hard cover : alk. paper)
1. Mississippi—Social life and customs—Anecdotes. 2. Mississippi—History, Local—Anecdotes. 3. Mississippi—Description and travel—Anecdotes. 4. Mississippi—Pictorial works. I. Title.
F341.6.G737 2010
976.2--dc22

2010031905

Printed in the USA at Walsworth Publishing Company

COVER PHOTO:

There could be many icons for Mississippi: Civil War cannons, the Ruins of Windsor, the Biloxi Lighthouse, and an endless number of Blues sites. But this is a good enough one, the heavenward-pointing hand on the steeple of Port Gibson Presbyterian Church. It's not your usual steeple. Just like Mississippians aren't your run-of-the-mill people. Maybe a little quirky to some folks. But good at heart, and headed in the right direction.

Contents

Preface

Wherever I go in Mississippi, whether to speak or shoot a story for WLBT or public television, usually someone will come up to me and tell me a story of some kind about someone in the area or about an old house or some funny instance that happened either to them or someone else. And when they finish telling me their tale, nine times out of ten I'll say something like, "Oh. That reminds me of. . . . ," and then I'll tell them a related story.

So when the Electric Power Associations of Mississippi decided to invite readers of their newspaper *Today in Mississippi* to send in their photographs of Mississippi, and asked me to write the narrative that would tie the pictures together, I looked forward to the task. I knew the pictures and the stories with them would be just the prompting I'd need to recall and jot down some more of the stories I've collected over the years while traveling the roads of Mississippi.

The following pages are what we came up with, you and I. A book with wonderful photography from people who love Mississippi and the folks who live here as well as the reason these photos are meaningful to the person who submitted them, as well as some of my observations about the subject at hand and life and living in Mississippi in general.

Hopefully, as you thumb through and look at the pictures and read the stories, all of this will remind you of stories you've heard (or lived) over the years. And as you tell someone about something you've seen in this book, it will prompt you to say, "Oh. That reminds me. . . . ," and you can tell a tale of your own.

Walt Grayson
May 2010

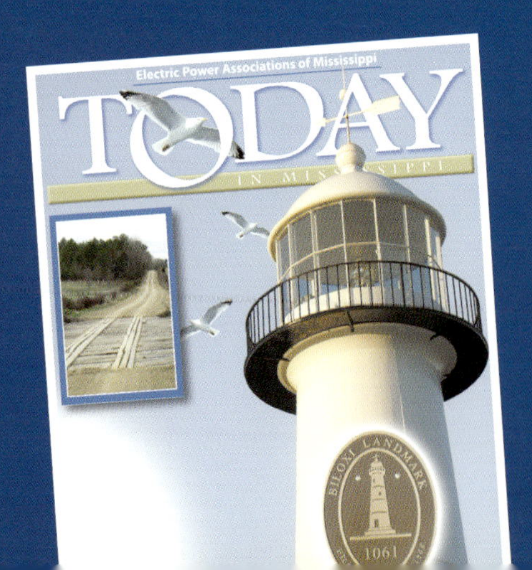

Thanks

to our loyal *Today in Mississippi* readers for allowing us to share their memories and photographs in this book. Like our readers' submissions, each issue of *Today in Mississippi* celebrates the beauty of life in the Magnolia State. Since 1948, the publication has reflected electric power associations' pride in their home state and their deep commitment to serving its people. *Today in Mississippi* has been a rural Mississippi tradition for more than sixty years, with a monthly circulation now topping 450,000.

hoto Credit: Clyde E. Gousset

Introduction

It was some type of brown pasteboard box, as I remember. Like a cigar box, only two or three times as large. And maybe it had a lip on the lid like you find on some Valentine candy boxes, so it fit snugly when closed. Maybe it even had a ribbon attached in such a fashion that it could be tied shut. I can't remember for sure. It's been too long ago. But I think that's what the box that held my family's treasure of photographs looked like. And although the look of the box is elusive in my memory, the contents aren't.

Mama and Daddy kept the box in the large storage cabinet that dropped down from the ceiling and ran from wall to wall over the bathtub in the bathroom off their bedroom. Christmas tree decorations and spare quilts and such were kept there, too, as well as the box full of pictures.

When I was big enough to climb on a chair and stand on the lavatory and get hold of the cabinet, but small enough to fold up into a pretty tight ball, the bathroom storage cabinet was just the right size for me to hide in when cousins came and on rainy days we had to play hide-and-seek inside the house.

When I'd stay home from school with a cold or something, oftentimes I'd haul down that box of pictures and look through them for entertainment. I had no idea who the people in the pictures were, except for just a few I recognized. But I knew they were all important, or we wouldn't have pictures of them.

(01) This is a photograph of my mother's family taken before I was born. And in case my grandkids ever see this book—yes, there was a time before I was born.

I must have pestered Mama half to death while she was trying to cook or iron, showing her fistfuls of photos and asking her who this was and who that was in single shots of old men and old women, babies, groups at family reunions, and even a few funerals.

They were mostly black-and-white pictures. Some had the squiggly Fox Photo borders around the edge that gave each shot a fancy printed-on frame. Some came in little yellow booklets. But most of them were just single photos that randomly stacked and reshuffled themselves like loose playing cards as the box was taken down and looked through and then replaced in the cabinet.

01

Each one of those photos was more than just a snapshot. Each represented a story. Sometimes a short story like, "Oh, that's Granddaddy Grayson standing in front of the house in Jackson after Frank left for the Army in World War II before Mama and the girls moved back to Fulton." Sometimes they were long stories. "Those are all the flowers on Granddaddy Cummings' grave when he died. He was well known in Itawamba County. Did I ever tell you about the time he. . . ." What would follow would be some ghost-busting story or a tall tale from Granddaddy's timber cruising days across Mississippi and Alabama and up into the foothills of the Smoky Mountains.

So I got to know photographs as more than just things. They were flashcards that opened up a story or a memory. They were containers that held the instance of joy or sadness or some other emotion evoked by the event they recorded. And as many sore throats as I had on cold, rainy, wintry Delta days back when I was a kid, I managed to get well acquainted with my family's collection of photographs we kept in the old box at our house.

I suppose looking through those old pictures is where photography started to appeal to me. I not only liked looking at the pictures, I knew I wanted to make pictures, too. I wanted to learn the mechanics of them as well as the art.

There were a bunch of negatives kept in that same box along with the photos. Most likely they were the negatives that some of the prints had been made from. On one of my sick days home from school, I decided I'd turn a negative into a print. I didn't know that the print wasn't somehow just a transformed negative. So I spent half a day squirting toothpaste and iodine and such things as that on one of the old negatives trying to turn it into a positive. I was sure I had almost unlocked the secret, but Mama caught me. It was a few decades later before I made my first prints in a makeshift darkroom at our college apartment.

It was after my daughter Keri was born. And the reason I got serious about making my own prints in my own darkroom was, it cost too much for a college family to keep taking the baby to have professional pictures done as often as we wanted them done. So I bought a 35mm camera and started taking my own pictures of her. I quickly branched out and took pictures of old buildings and cemeteries and nature scenes and the like.

I covered the tiny window in the shower of the bathroom in our apartment at Mississippi College in Clinton, which easily converted it into a darkroom. I'd go to class in the mornings, go to work in the afternoon and evening, and then at night after I got off work, I'd set up my enlarger and chemical trays and develop pictures. By the way, making prints from negatives has nothing to do with toothpaste, I discovered.

I was working at WSLI-FM in Jackson at the time. It was called Jackson Family Radio back then—all Christian music and programming all the time. Mike Dana and I and an automation machine ran the station twenty-four hours a day. I'd go in to work after classes and monitor the automation machine until some point in the afternoon (I forget exactly when—4:00 p.m., probably), and then go live until 10:00 p.m. when I got off work. Then I would load up the automation machine to run the station overnight until Mike got there the next morning at 6:00 a.m.

Some days when I got to work, there would be things I would need to do, such as make commercials or record more records onto the big reels of tape that ran on the automation machine when no one was there. But lots of days, there was nothing to do but wait until 4:00 p.m. for my live shift.

Mike Dana was also a photography buff, as well as Lee O'Quinn, who worked the afternoon shift on the AM station in the room next door. Lee had been into photography a lot longer than Mike and I had been, and Lee had bought an entire set of photographic encyclopedias. When Lee discovered Mike's and my interest in the subject, Lee brought all those books up to the radio station for us to thumb through.

The books told about shutter speed and how various speeds affected a photograph. Then it went into lens aperture and explained that how wide the lens was open affected depth of field. And the books broached the subjects of filters for black-and-white and color photography, and how they modified reality to make the photo look more like what you envisioned and to capture the emotion of the scene than just an unmodified photograph could. There were examples of composition and creating mood.

So at the same time I was getting a degree from Mississippi College in my morning classes, I was also learning a great deal about photography from Lee O'Quinn's encyclopedias in the afternoon at work waiting my turn to go on the air.

Sometimes Lee would bring his leftover photographic print paper for either Mike or me to use in our darkrooms at home. A box of one hundred sheets of photo print paper looks sort of like the box a fine book might come in and is wrapped in heavy, light-proof black plastic inside to keep the paper from being accidentally exposed.

One day Lee set the remainder of a box of five-by-seven-inch paper on the desk in the FM room for whichever of us got to it first. (Keep in mind that our FM station was religious at that time.) So later that day, after Mike discovered the box of photo print paper, he went into the AM control room and thanked Lee for bringing that new Bible for us, all boxed up so nice. But Mike told him the printer must have made a mistake because all the pages were blank. Lee gasped until he realized Mike was joking.

Our State the Way We See It

Why do we take pictures of all the things we choose to take pictures of? Beautiful sunsets, family, friends, and places we've been? Obviously, there is something in the scene in front of us that we want to try to preserve. And it isn't just the look of it that is important to us. But also it's the feel of it and what we were thinking at the time we snapped the shutter; those are also the things we want to hold onto. And just as a smell or a taste can take you back to your childhood—a whiff of honeysuckle can carry you back to a youthful sunny summer day, or the aroma of bacon cooking can carry you back to breakfast at grandmother's, a photograph can take you right back to where you were the day you snapped it. And years later, other people who weren't even there when it was taken, looking at the same picture, can feel some of the same emotions that are captured in it.

When I run across pictures of family reunions from way before I was even born—all the family in dress-up clothes posed in front of the old family home, husbands standing behind wives—it gives me a snug, secure feeling of belonging. I can see photographs of landscapes and get the sense of grandeur that the scene before the camera expressed.

So in the following pictures, as you look at them, we're taking in not only what the photographer saw, but we'll also get a sense of why they took that photo in the first place; why they wanted us to see this particular scene.

One more thought before we dive into the pictures. Years ago I did a story about the "Splendors of Versailles" exhibit in Jackson. I opened the story with a sentence something to the effect of, "If aliens from another planet were to land on Earth, this is one of the places we'd be sure to take them and show to them." I sort of get that idea about photographs. Not that we're likely to have visitors from other worlds land here and want to thumb through our photo albums, but these pictures are often good times captured to be shared with folks who weren't there at the time to experience what we were seeing when we snapped the picture. My TV series *Look Around Mississippi* is built around that same idea; for me to be the eyes of people who can't be where I am, and likely never will get to see what I am seeing.

So we have a rare privilege in the following pages, to be somewhere we were not, and see wonderful things through other people's eyes, and feel what they felt and enjoy what they enjoyed.

Now, let's get to the photographs.

(02) The first picture comes to us from Mac H. Alford of Hattiesburg. He snapped this shot where Highway 15 ends at Highway 26 between Wiggins and Lucedale. Jo and I have stopped at the spot many times to admire exactly what Mac snapped his picture of the pitcher plants. Here is what Mac has to say about this shot:

— Mac: Mississippi's coastal plain is rich in meat-eating plants, and these pitcher plants (*Sarracenia alata*) are common and beautiful elements of the longleaf pine savanna. Buttercup Flats always surprises me with its diversity of unusual little plants.

02

— Walt: Jo and I first ran across Buttercup Flats as we were coming back from doing a story on the coast and were trying to find a Stone County cemetery that had wooden grave markers. History Professor Emeritus at Gulf Coast Community College, Perkinston Campus, Charles Sullivan had mentioned the unusual grave markers and told me approximately where to find them. On the way to search for the cemetery, we bumped into acres and acres of pitcher plants on the north side of Highway 26. We don't have anything like pitcher plants in the central part of the state and northward, so the odd-shaped bug catchers fascinated us.

One year, we tried to set some pitcher plants out in the wet area near the little pond that overlaps into my yard from my neighbor's yard. But about the time we set them out, the neighbor, in an effort to keep the pond weed-free, sprayed weed killer on everything around. So we *still* don't know if they will grow this far north in the state.

(03) The next four photos were submitted by Angela L. Martin from Hazlehurst. She says:

— Angela: All of these photos were taken by me on our property here in Copiah County. This is what I see each year, the beauty. I wrote a poem as a young girl and revised it three years ago for submission to be published. The title of the poem is "Nature, The Art of God." To me, these photographs explain the words in my poem explicitly. What an awesome artist we can know personally. An artist that needs no brush, just a spoken word and the beauty came forth for all the world to see. . . .

03

"He that dwelleth in the secret place of the Most High shall abide under the shadow of the Almighty." Psalm 91:1

— Walt: The snowfall in Angela's photo is from early December 2008. Our youngest granddaughter had just turned nine years old in November 2008 and had never seen snow up until then. By the time she was ten, she had seen about five good snows. I don't know what that says about global warming, if anything. But it reminds me of my childhood in Mississippi. I think I was at least nine or so years old before it snowed in Greenville. But when it started, it started! Including the six-inch snow we had on the ground on Christmas Day 1962, and a few particularly deep freezes over the next few winters.

04

I guess it snowed regularly every winter until I graduated high school in the late 1960s, and then it slowed until it finally gave us one last good snow about 1984. Then came the long dry spell until 2008 with the exception of a few spits and spurts that didn't amount to too much. Then in 2008, it started snowing again in Mississippi.

06

(04, 05, 06) Angela's pictures go on to show spring flowers and a summer butterfly and a barn in autumn with some mums in the foreground.

Speaking of barns, I can't think of where all that many barns are anymore in Mississippi. I know of some. Mr. Brewer Browning's barn, for instance, in north Madison County. Brewer has been gone for some time now. But years and years ago, he told me that when he and his wife, Robbie Lee, first married and bought land, the barn was the first thing they built. Then they built their house.

There is the big barn south of Grenada on Highway 51, the red barn south of Rolling Fork on Highway 61, the round barns near Blue Mountain way up north. I know of a set of wonderful barns in Copiah County, if their upkeep hasn't caused their downfall by now.

05

(07) This photo is a shot of the red barn on Highway 61 south of Rolling Fork I snapped one day on the way home from shooting a *Look Around Mississippi* story farther up the road at Lake Washington.

I know where more barns used to be than still are. Times and needs change. But barns represent stability and security. I'm not sure what we've replaced them with. Not a garage. That's just a place to keep a car, or stuff you don't want to haul into the attic.

Maybe that's one reason we feel so insecure nowadays. We don't have anything tangible like a barn where we can physically see that our provisions for our future are safe and cared for. Barns were the shelter for the implements that made a living, and where surplus material was stockpiled until needed, and food stored, and the animals that help grow that food sheltered. We don't have a modern-day equivalent for a barn except maybe our checkbooks.

(08) The next photo is of the Beverly Drive-In Theatre in Hattiesburg. Ashley Campbell sent it in. This is one of two photos of the Beverly we received. The other comes later in the book. Ashley says of her picture:

— Ashley: This is a part of history that should be restored and begun running again. The theatre originally opened in 1948 and reopened in 2001, but I never have had a chance to experience this. I think it would be a lot of fun to go back in time to see how our grandparents watched movies.

07

— Walt: Oh baby! That last line hurts! Ms. Jo and I had our first date at a drive-in movie in Greenville! 'Course, we are grandparents now. So I guess Angela's time placement of drive-in movie theatres is accurate.

I thought it was odd that Jo's parents let us go to the drive-in for several reasons. First of all, I had just gotten my driver's license not all that long before then. Plus, it was a drive-in, and we'd be alone. But mainly the drive-in was in competition with where Jo's dad worked, the walk-in Paramount Theatre in downtown Greenville. But the movie was the Beatles' *A Hard Day's Night* and was only going to be shown at the drive-in, so it was special enough that Jo's mom and dad let us go. And silly us, we were so young that all we did was watch the movie.

08

(09) The next photo looks a lot like some of the ones in Mama and Daddy's stash of photographs that I looked through when I was a youngster; black and white, unposed. Just taken. And obviously this shot is from a good while back. This is a good example of a picture not being just a picture, but telling a story.

Faye Vinson Bordelon of Hattiesburg sent in this one. She calls it, "John Vinson with children piled on his 1949 DeSoto, Meehan, MS, 1952." And this is what comes to her mind when she sees it:

— Fay: Four of the children pictured with my father, John Vinson, belong to him. The older girl is my cousin, Phyllis Tarifa, who looked up to my father as her own. The boy with his back to the camera is my cousin, Billy Gatlin, from Meehan. I am the girl looking toward the camera. We are at my maternal grandparents' home, after traveling up Highway 11 from New Orleans with my paternal grandmother, my mother, and Phyllis.

Daddy built a bench the same height as the backseat of the DeSoto. Then he helped Mama pile quilts and blankets over both the bench and the seat. He drove to Meridian at night, while all us noisy children snoozed on our car bed. A smart man!

09

Daddy and Mama (Connie Gatlin) were hastily married at Indianola on September 24, 1942, the day he was scheduled to report for duty in World War II. Even though he spent three and a half years in New Guinea, their union, unlike many rushed into at the time, lasted until he died in 1996. On her last anniversary, Mama put a note on the skirt she was wearing when Daddy came and took her out of her math class at Moorhead High School. Poor Mama. When she dressed that morning, she had no idea that she was donning her wedding attire. She said they had sewn the skirt by lamplight from material that cost less than a dollar. She then wrote that they "traveled to Indianola in a truck, Daddy in work clothes and I in my priceless skirt." There are no pictures of them that day. I first saw the skirt after her death in 2001.

Two innocents from the Delta were thrust into an even harder existence, but they always drew strength from their roots.

— Walt: After Mama died, we found the old photos from my childhood in the bottom of a box a vacuum cleaner had come in, under several pieces of polyester material from the 1970s, in the bottom of a closet in her home in Fulton. We five kids divided the pictures. I see one of the photos pop up on Facebook on one of my brothers' or sisters' pages now and again.

I think it is too bad that our kids and grandkids didn't have those kinds of pictures to rummage through when they stayed home sick from school on a rainy day, so they would know where they came from, like Faye and her story about that picture she sent in.

I don't intend for this to turn into a "These Kids These Days" kind of book, but from the old family pictures, I have always been aware that I belonged to something bigger than just myself. I got an idea early on life of what a family was and how *big* it was, and that there were more people involved in the outcome of my life than just me. And most important, although it was hard to imagine by looking at them in person, those "old folks" I lived with were once as young as I was, and they seemed to have had no better sense when they were young than I did at the time, and they turned out okay. But they did so partly because they knew they would be letting a lot of people down if they *didn't* turn out okay. They knew that because they had seen the pictures of all those people, just as I had.

(10) The picture of the little church comes to us from Aubrey Harris of Glen Allan in Washington County in the Delta. He titles it "Old Mayersville Methodist Church at Its New Home." Here's what Aubrey says of this beautiful photo.

— Aubrey: Wonderful friends of mine, John Allen and Eileen Darnell, now deceased, told me about this church. They had a picture (a painting, I think, hanging on the wall of their home) of the original structure as it stood in Mayersville, Issaquena County, and attended the church from childhood to adulthood. Its beauty is striking, and its history is quite interesting. I was told by the Darnells that the Methodist Church in Mayersville was closed, and at some time after its closure, the Lakeland Presbyterian Church (in Flowood, an adjoining suburb of Jackson) bought the structure and moved it to its current location.

I have not attempted to verify the information told me by the Darnells, but I believe it is true.

10

— Walt: Thank you, Aubrey, for the picture and the story behind it. I haven't checked on all the particulars either, but that's the gist of the story that I heard about the little church when it popped up on top of the first hill east of the Jackson airport on Lakeland Drive. Only I had heard that the church came from Glen Allan. But since Aubrey lives in Glen Allan, he'd know better than I.

I joke that I rarely ever bother to check on the validity of a story that anyone tells me, because it might prove to be inaccurate and then I wouldn't get to use it. I don't mean to imply that I make stuff up. But I do go a lot by just what other people tell me.

For instance, after we had run another haunted house story on *Look Around Mississippi* on WLBT one afternoon, veteran news anchor Bert Case turned to me on the air and point blank asked me if I believed there was really any such thing as ghosts. So I explained to him that technically in that story, I wasn't the one who claimed there was a ghost in the house. It was the people who owned the place that made that statement. I just simply put them on the air saying it.

If we had to stick strictly to accuracy in our stories, Daddy would have never walked to school so many times in the snow when he was a boy. (In the Louisiana Delta?) But the bigger point he was trying to make by telling the story was worth the fabrication.

Somebody asked one of my favorite storytellers (maybe it was Willie Morris, could have been Jerry Clower, or maybe even Mark Twain) if everything he had said in a particular story was true. The response was, it may not have all been true, but it all was *truth*.

Speaking of Mayersville, you can always tell when a new weather person or news reporter hits our area. First time they run up on the name Mayersville, they'll pronounce it *Mayor's*-ville instead of *Myers*-ville. (Similarly, Belzoni becomes Belzon-e a few times until someone sets them straight.)

(11) The next picture is another that Aubrey Harris from Glen Allan sent in. "The Old Cotton House at Chatham, Mississippi" is just up Lake Washington from Glen Allan. Aubrey says of this one:

11

— Aubrey: Cotton has been the "white gold" of the Mississippi Delta. This structure stands as another landmark for the area. It was part of an old gin plant operated by the Steins (probably constructed in the 1920s or 1930s—uncertain about the exact time of its construction and operation). The time was certainly when farming was done with mules and hand labor. The gin plant with its other associated structures, e.g., seed house, is long gone. Only some foundation structures of the gin can be seen, but the old round cotton house still stands. The purpose of this round cotton house was for the gin's farmer customers to store cotton when more cotton was being harvested and transported to the gin than the gin could process in a timely manner. A mule-drawn cotton wagon could carry enough raw cotton to turn out one bale of lint. When a wagonload of cotton arrived at the gin and there were too many wagons ahead of it for ginning, the driver would be directed to temporarily place his load in one of the pie-shaped compartments of the round house (cotton house). It could then be ginned later, and the driver could return to the farm for another load. The gin probably processed two or four bales an hour, a much slower pace than modern gins.

— Walt: From way back in my boyhood I still have memories of the old way of growing cotton. Daddy worked all over the Delta, and I went to work with him many days. And in the summer there would be field hands in the hot sun chopping cotton. In the fall, they would be hand picking with long cotton sacks dragging the ground behind them, all in a long line in a row from one side of the field to the other.

Then, mechanization came in. We did a *Mississippi Roads* story with a longtime planter in the northern part of the Delta one Sunday morning. We were around Marks somewhere.

He told us that back in the 1950s, it took ten families full time to take care of a hundred acres of cotton. Now, he said one man on a tractor could take care of that hundred acres by himself in no time at all. But the families were still living in the Delta with nothing to do.

And that's the story of the Delta. Little towns like Arcola and Anguilla and Sunflower and Drew and dozens more once thrived as "furnish" centers for the plantations and the workers. But as mechanization took over, the need for such places evaporated.

Nowadays, the Delta is one of the richest poorest places in the nation. How do you fix it? I'm not that smart. I guess nobody is, because it ain't fixed yet. But it seems to me that when you are sitting on the richest farmland on the planet, the solution to the Delta has to come from utilizing that resource and growing things.

(12) Natasha Bane sent in the next photo. Title: "Swinging Bridge."

This bridge is in Byram just south of Jackson off I-55. Natasha says of her subject:

— Natasha: I have lived in Mississippi all my life and in the Byram area for over thirty-five years. The swinging bridge was built in 1905, I was told, by a local blacksmith. It's a shame it has not been kept up any better than it has.

— Walt: I have driven across this bridge. Not lately, but when it was *the* bridge between Byram and Florence. A fully loaded tanker truck ended that one night, trying to take a shortcut between Interstate 55 and Highway 49. It was several tons more than the wooden bed suspended from cables could handle. With one mighty groan, Hinds and Rankin Counties had to move from the Model T to the modern age when forced to build a new bridge about a hundred or so yards up the Pearl River from the old swinging bridge.

It was a great adventure to cross the old bridge. It was only one lane, for starters. And if you wanted to scare your passengers, you took it real fast. If you *really* wanted to scare them, you took it r-e-a-l-l-y slow! Creeping across the bridge, you heard every board creak and moan as if they were about to give way, as your tires rolled across them and jarred them.

12

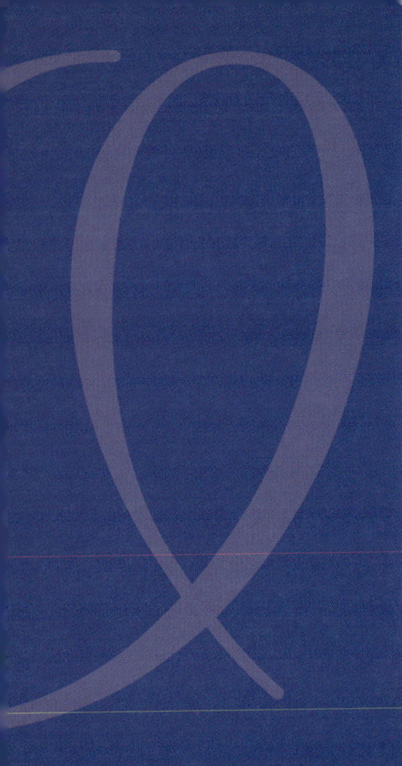

13

Florence Upton of Brandon told me her grandfather supervised the building of that bridge. She said he had worked on the Brooklyn Bridge in New York.

With the closing of the Byram swinging bridge went the end of an era. I was told at one time there were over a hundred similar bridges in Mississippi. The one at Byram was the last in operation.

(13) Rebecca (Becca) McMillan brings us to a haunting category with our next photograph, old churches. She says this one is next to the house on the hill in Rolling Fork. No doubt she's referring to Mont Helena, built on top of an Indian mound just north of town. She calls this picture "Abandoned Church." And she says of it:

— Becca: The old abandoned church caught my eye. Every place in Mississippi has several churches. This one was abandoned. I have to wonder—where did the congregation go? How many souls were saved in that church?

— Walt: Oh Lawdy! Old churches! The mind reels. Old-time religion is what we were all brought up on, if we were lucky. Probably didn't think so at the time. I come from a very religious family. While they were fixing breakfast at family reunions, my aunts could get into an argument over which denomination was going to be the Bride of Christ and which ones were only going to be the bridesmaids at the Second Coming. To confuse matters, I had an Uncle Lloyd. And in the northeast Mississippi brogue they all spoke in, it was hard to determine if someone was referring to "The Lord" or "Lloyd" sometimes. Both sounded almost the same. And both came up in conversation often.

(14) Becca also sent in the next photograph. It is a picture of the piano left behind in the abandoned church. She says of it:

— Becca: This piano was in the abandoned church. The keys are all messed up. It sits right next to the window where the sun always shines. I'm sure someone used the piano to play a lot of hymns in worship.

14

15

(15) Here's another old church. I was actually invited to speak at this church one Sunday morning. I'll say more about the church after we read what Billy Buford of Brookhaven has to say about it. He submitted the photograph.

— Billy: Franklin Presbyterian Church is located east of Highway 17 between Pickens and Lexington. The church, not now active, was in existence prior to the Civil War as evidenced by several cannonball holes in the structure. The church is special to my family as it was the home church for my maternal great-great-grandparents. My great-great-grandfather Thomas B. Owen was buried here in 1900 and his wife Ella Bush Owen in 1932. There are numerous very old grave markers in the church cemetery, many of which are shaped like tree trunks, which was a death benefit of Woodman of the World members long ago.

— Walt: The Sunday I spoke there they were having the annual homecoming service followed by dinner on the grounds. Fortunately, there was someone in the congregation who knew a great deal more than I did about the Civil War battle that took place at the church. And there are still holes in the wood siding from projectiles about the size of grapeshot (a little bigger than a lemon) attesting to the fact that war was waged there. The story goes that people from the community hid under the church to get away from the fighting.

Some of the dead buried in the cemetery are from the battle. I understand the drummer boy for one side or the other was killed in the fighting and is buried here.

One of the more interesting tombstones details the death of a man killed by his best friend with whom he had gone into business. Things must have gone bad, and a duel resulted, and the tombstone resulted from the duel. Quite a poem is engraved on the tombstone telling the whole story and advising friends not to go into business with each other.

Someone from nearby Lexington told me he took a troop of Cub Scouts out to see the church and the cemetery a while back. As the boys somberly went from grave to grave looking at the epitaphs and the names and the dates, one puzzled boy spoke up and asked why they put this guy's phone number on his tombstone. "Phone number?" the man asked. "Yea, 1 834-1901." The prefix for Lexington phone numbers is 834. The youngster figured the death date of 1834 was the beginning of a phone number with the "1" added like it was a long distance call. (And I guess it would be to get in touch with the deceased wherever he is now.)

Mis

(16) The next picture was sent in by Robert R. Robida of Olive Branch. Robert calls this photo, "Job Abandoned, Work Undone." And he says of it:

— Robert: It is part of a series of homes I photographed when I came across them. This house used to stand on Church Road, heading toward I-55, but before getting to I-55 in Southhaven, Mississippi. This home stood diagonally across from a church on the hill with a cemetery attached. After I moved here (January 2009), every time I passed this house I said to myself, "I have to get a photo of this house." One Sunday, after church, I stopped and did photograph this house. I have this very shot in a few versions: One is simply black and white. Another is full color. Another is enhanced color, and this one is black and white with some color restored. Once I restored some of the color, it looked like a house someone had started to fix up, and then abandoned. Hence, the title of this photo. Sadly, this house is no longer standing. One day, when I drove by, I noticed it was gone. Must have been torn down.

16

— Walt: Good for you for stopping and getting the shot while there was still a shot to get! I have lost a few of what I considered would have been great photographs because I procrastinated too long, figuring I had all the time in the world to get it. Meanwhile, the building was torn down or burned down or something before I ever dragged my lazy self out of the car to frame and focus and snap.

Two other instances come to mind of stories that I missed because I waited too long. Ethel Wright Mohammed of Belzoni was a late-blooming (or better put, late-recognized) folk artist. Mrs. Mohammed stitched scenes onto pillowcases of places in Belzoni and also illustrated stories that had taken place in the Mohammed household; Christmas morning, for example. Some of her work is now a part of the Smithsonian permanent collection.

While she was still living, she had turned her home into a showplace to display her collection of stitched pillowcases. For years I realized Ms. Mohamed was just up the road and knew that all I ever had to do to get her story was to call her up and drive to Belzoni. But I figured her story was a given. I could do it any time. I'd do the hard stories first and save Ms. Mohammed for a day when I couldn't find anything else.

So you can just about imagine my shock when I picked up the Clarion-Ledger one morning and read the front-page headline that she had passed away.

I did the story of her collection later with Mrs. Mohammed's daughter, Joy, conducting the tour. (Now Joy has passed away, too. So I am glad I got her, at least.) I enjoyed the way the story turned out with Joy inserting all of her love and admiration for her mother, but I would have really loved to have done a story with Ethel Wright Mohammed herself. And could have, except for procrastination.

17

Similarly, Willie Morris suggested he and I go to Yazoo City and let him give me a tour of all the important places: the Witch's Grave, where Skip was buried, the Confederate shipyard, and places where he hung out with his friends as a child. We both agreed it was a wonderful idea and we'd do it as soon as we both found the time. Then Willie died.

Willie Morris giving a tour of Yazoo City on video would be just about as valuable as Lincoln giving a tour of the Gettysburg Battlefield. Well, almost as valuable.

Jesus tried to warn us that, "The thief comes to kill, steal and destroy." And one of his best plans to accomplish this is procrastination. Two good stories I let be stolen from me because I didn't make hay while the sun was shining.

(17) Alex Bonner from Panama City, Florida, sent us a picture of the Hickory water tower. His title for it is, "Hickory Water Tower, 6:00 a.m." About the photo he says:

— Alex: Shot of the water tower in downtown Hickory. It was a quiet morning indicative of a quiet Mississippi town.

— Walt: When I first saw this picture, I thought it was taken just after sunset. It could have been. Same shadows, same highlighted clouds, only the light at sunset would have been coming from the opposite direction. That reminded me of a story I aired a few years ago of several sunsets. I probably wrote something I figured was just this side of profound and maybe just the other side of poetic to tie them all together. And then I picked a tranquil piece of music and edited the dissolves between the sunsets in time with the music.

After the story aired, I walked from the studio back into the newsroom and one of the producers complimented me on my beautiful sunrises. I suppose it was the way I was searching for words to thank her for the compliment that must have tipped her off that I was a late sleeper, because she suddenly corrected herself, saying, "Oh. Those were sunsets, weren't they?"

(18) Patsy Brewer, who is the library director at the Waynesboro-Wayne County Library, sent the next photograph and gave it two titles. One: "The Road More Traveled." And two: "Fallen Snow." She says of her picture:

— Patsy: This photo was taken the day it snowed at our house. Since snow in our area is rare, it makes this road to be the road *more* traveled because of its beauty instead of the road *less* traveled.

— Walt: I am glad we live in a part of the world where we can say, "This was made *the* day it snowed," and everyone knows what day that was. Because it just doesn't snow all that much here.

When I was growing up, I loved snow. But it was only after I was out in the world a few years that I fully understood why. Because when you are a kid and it snows, you get out of school! When you are grown up and it snows, it only makes your work harder, especially if you are a weather reporter in broadcasting.

But snow is such a rarity in Mississippi that few of us ever outgrow getting excited when we see the first flakes start falling. It snows so infrequently that I think I can remember every snow we've had. I *know* I remember all of the major snows. But now that I think about it, I may be rolling later ice storm memories into the snow memories of events like the big Christmas snow of 1962. That was my first white Christmas. And frankly, I didn't like it all that much.

18

Oh, it was pretty, all right. But it was Christmas Day, and we had outdoor toys to play with and couldn't because it was so cold. The biggest thing we did that day was, my older brother David and I walked through the side yard kicking up snow.

Snows are big media events in Mississippi. When I was working in radio, we all assumed we grew very important during snow events, passing along traffic and weather updates. Television was even better, especially in the years when I was doing weather.

19

Early in my career at WLBT, our competitor had hired a pretty good weather guy from Michigan. For an out-of-towner, he even nailed the proper pronunciations of Belzoni and Kosciusko. But his downfall came when snow was in the forecast. But he reported for us not to worry. It would only be a couple of inches. "Only" and "a couple of inches" don't go in the same sentence when you are talking about a Mississippi snow! That's enough to grind Jackson to a halt! State government shuts down at *one* inch! I think he moved to a Florida TV station next.

(19) Jack Brumfield of Tylertown took the picture of the sunset at Lake Walthall, and he titled it, "Sunset over Walthall." And he says of it:

— Jack: Everybody who loves the outdoors has been to a state lake at one time or another. This is a photo of one I enjoy going to.

— Walt: Now this picture is as pretty as a picture. The color in the cloud is echoed by the mirror-smooth lake, separated by the trees; trees already melted into one by the fleeting light. About this time of evening, the birds are settling for the night and the katydids are beginning to sing along with the crickets.

Sunsets were my specialty with my first camera. It wasn't a fancy camera, but we were on a "plan" where we got free film returned to us with every processing order. All of that came along with a family album bound in genuine leather-looking plastic. This plan and accompanying photo album were sold to us in the first month after our wedding by a door-to-door salesman who, no doubt, scoured the wedding announcements in the newspaper for leads. Here we could hardly buy groceries and yet let this guy sell us this family album and film processing deal on time installments.

All these years later, the picture album is still upstairs in a closet. It lasted longer than the marriage. It has pictures in it from that first family and the blended family that has been mine since then—as well as maybe one or two of those sunset shots I took off the levee in Greenville all those years ago.

What is it about a sunset that we like? Well, what's not to like? The color, the quietness—then there are the intangibles like the assessments we make of ourselves at the ending of another day and the beginning of night.

My Aunt Coleen was talking about family when we visited with her recently. She is the last one of her brothers and sisters still living. She was telling us how she and my mother, who was the youngest and closest in age to Aunt Coleen, grew to be great friends over the years. And how that after Daddy retired and he and Mama moved into the house directly across the street from Aunt Coleen in Fulton, Mama would come and get her and make her come outside and look if there was a pretty sunset.

20

(20) The next four pictures come from Shelley Putnam Burge of the Dixie Community in Forrest County south of Hattiesburg. Of the first one, the boy in the creek, she says:

— Shelley: This image was shot in 2007 on an annual Fourth of July camping trip our friends and their families take to Cypress Creek in Perry County. Branson, who was about nine at this time, is typically a very active and energetic young boy. This moment intrigued me because he, like all the adults on the trip, was able to relax and enjoy the simple beauty of Mississippi as he sat on a slippery soapstone and listened to the sound of the rushing water in the distance.

— Walt: Mississippi has some great creeks in the southern part of the state below Hattiesburg. Well, we have great creeks in other places, too. But the ones below Hattiesburg have a distinctive quality to them. For one thing, their water is clear. Well, clear-*ish*. It would be clear except for the tannic acid that gives creeks like Red Creek and Black Creek and this one, Cypress Creek, their color. The tannic acid comes from decaying vegetation that has fallen into the creeks. Many of the creeks have been developed for canoeing. Forty miles of Black Creek flowing through the DeSoto National Forest is Mississippi's only National Scenic River. And since it is in a national forest, it is open to the public.

I had been invited to speak to the annual Chamber of Commerce banquet at Wiggins a year or so ago. I told them when they invited me that it sure would be nice if there was a story I could do while I was there. Our schedule stays so tight with story deadlines that it's hard to just go somewhere without doing a story while we're there.

So the folks at Wiggins lined up John Bond, who floats and fishes the Red Creek a good bit, to take Jo and me on a three-hour cruise downstream so I could get some shots to use for a *Mississippi Roads* segment.

Robin Lott, who works with John, took the afternoon off to give Ms. Jo some company. So off we went. John explained that the folks around Wiggins wanted to develop the creek for float trips much like Red Creek and Okatoma Creek had been developed.

Not long after shoving off and getting into the current so it could carry us, John and Robin came out with fishing poles. I declined joining in on the fishing because I already had plenty to do trying to steady a video camera to get shots of the sand bars and show the way the water changes colors when a side creek empties into the main channel and how far below the surface you could see logs and stuff. But Ms. Jo didn't want to just sit there while I worked and they fished, so she took up the offer to wet a hook and see if she could catch anything.

So here I am concentrating on the scene in my viewfinder when all of a sudden from behind me comes the "whizz" of a spinning reel and in front of me goes a "plop" as a lure lands right in the middle of the video frame I am shooting. Then for the next little while it seemed that every shot I was trying to take had either a rod tip rushing through it or a splash of a lure finding water in it somewhere. But I figured I could edit around all those interruptions since I was shooting lots and lots of footage.

But when I got back home and started looking over my video, there were very few complete scenes that didn't have an actual fishing rod in the picture or at least the plop of a lure in the audio. Or girly squealing as Jo caught a fish.

It turned out that I had to make the story about *fishing* Red Creek instead of *floating* Red Creek.

So to see young Branson sitting in the water all contemplative like that reminds me of the story I *wanted* to do about Red Creek. Now, imagine a brass band playing loudly all around him and you get an idea of the story I ended up with.

(21) For the mailbox photo Shelley says:

— Shelley: I took this image a few months ago near my home in the Dixie community south of Hattiesburg. These mailboxes belong to a mobile home park set far off the road. From the road, the only evidence that the park exists is this row of mailboxes, which, until recently, weren't very noticeable. But the Smiths moved in, and all that has changed! I love the fact that they have made their mailbox stand out by painting it Deer Huntin' Orange. Only in Mississippi!

— Walt: I don't know that I'd want my mailbox to stand out from the rest. Mine already attracts too many bills and too much junk mail as it is.

21

23

22

I was trying to think if there was a story I had ever done about mailboxes. The only one I recall was when I was on the coast doing an interview for Mississippi Public Broadcasting's *Beyond Katrina* series. Suzanne Shifalo was the expert I was talking to for the MPB story. We had picked a place not too far from the beach in Bay St. Louis to use as a background. There was nothing left standing there. All you could see were just slabs where houses used to be in every direction.

Her husband, Jesse, brought her to the location and told her he'd be right back. He said since they were that close to where their house used to be that he'd go check the mailbox. It was a few minutes into the interview before it dawned on me what Jesse had said. Check the mailbox?

Suzanne explained that the only thing left standing for three blocks inland on their street was their mailbox. And that as soon as the debris had been cleared enough to drive on that street again, the Post Office resumed delivering mail to their mailbox. There was no house there—matter of fact, no houses within sight almost—just their mailbox, dutifully filled with mail every day by the Postal Service.

So not only did the mailbox survive, it still functioned!

(22) For the Purple Field photo she says:

— Shelley: I took this image in March 2009 when our church (Dixie Baptist, Hattiesburg area) planted a garden of corn, tomatoes, and squash with our preschoolers. The kids had a ball digging in the dirt, but when they had had their fill of planting, a few of them went for a "hike." How precious to watch these young friends visit in this masterpiece of breathtakingly colorful weeds beside the church.

— Walt: Not that the purple flowers aren't pretty, but it's the kids walking through them that makes the picture. What a sweet age. I remember one day as I was playing in my sand pile, Daddy told me to stay a kid as long as I could. That's all I remember about the situation. But now I wonder what was going on in his life for him to come out with that particular piece of advice at that particular time?

Like an idiot, I didn't do it and couldn't *wait* to grow up. I got married right out of high school and took off for the bright lights of the big city (Jackson) the next year.

Way, way later in life, I gave my daughter Keri the same advice. She just turned thirty-five years old, and in the latest photograph of herself that she emailed to me, she is dressed as the worm from Jim Henson's movie *Labyrinth*. It was screening at the Mississippi Museum of Art recently, and the public was invited to come see it dressed as their favorite character. Not that Keri isn't responsibly employed overseeing a whole department at MPB television—but we're *still* waiting to see what she's going to be when she finally *does* grow up!

(23) Shelley says of the watermelon bucket photo:

— Shelley: Our church (Dixie Baptist, Hattiesburg area) held its first annual Patriotic Celebration in 2009. Among the festivities on the boiling hot day were a hot-dog-eating contest, a watermelon-seed-spitting contest, and water fun. To beat the heat, these two best friends squeezed themselves into a water-filled bucket with their watermelon in hand.

— Walt: I did a story about the watermelon-seed-spitting contest in Mize one summer. There were melons of all shapes and sizes at the festival. Just before the seed spit, there was a watermelon-eating contest. I think a twelve-year-old girl won it—and not a big girl, either.

The spitting contest I would have *liked* to have done a story about had long since ceased being held by the time I started doing TV features. The National Tobacco Spitting contest had been held annually at Billy John Crumpton's farm outside Raleigh for a while. Now that would have made a juicy story.

(24) Don Cane of Louisville sent the pictures of the bluebird, the tree roots, the lightning, and of Sciple's Mill. He says:

24

— Don: The photo of the bluebird was taken May 31, 2004. The bluebird house is about thirty feet from the back window of our house. I noticed the activity of the birds flying in and out. I set my camera in the window and started shooting. Many shots were made before getting the full spread of the wings. These little birds are fast, and you can't see this when they are landing.

— Walt: I call these perfect shots like the one of the bluebird in flight, and later, the lightning, a "lucky dog" shot. And when I get something that qualifies as one, I skip up and down and put on a cartoon voice and sing, "Oh, I'm a lucky dog. I'm a lucky dog." But it's not luck, really. It's a combination of skill and talent and knowing what you are looking for, and a little smidge of being in the right place at the right time doesn't hurt. You don't just walk up to a birdhouse and snap a shot like this.

(25) As far as the tree roots, Don says:

— Don: The photo of roots was taken November 12, 2005, below the spillway at the Noxubee Wildlife Refuge.

— Walt: Someone asked the great photographer Ansel Adams what was the most important element in taking a great photograph. He replied, "You have to know where to set the camera." Don's camera capturing the roots is set in just the right place. No telling how many other people in general and photographers in particular would pass right by

25

that same set of roots and never pay any attention to it. But Don captured the tangled mass that, when put in context with the ground and the water and the tree trunk, makes a wonderful picture.

(26) The photo of the lightning intrigues me. Don says of it:

— Don: The photo of the lightning was taken during a thunderstorm one night in 2007. Many unsuccessful attempts were made before this success. Fortunately, this was a very active thunderstorm, and I had many opportunities. Persistence paid off. You only have a split second to make this photo. With my camera on a tripod and the shutter held open, I waited for the right time to close the shutter and, with luck, make this photo. My camera was set up next to my house facing east toward my neighbor's house about six hundred yards away. That's the neighbor's house in the photo.

— Walt: The lightning shot is like the bluebird shot in that it takes a good bit of photographic skill to get it, but a great deal more luck than with the bluebird because lightning is random and can more easily strike outside the area where the camera is focused

than within it. If you want to get a shot of lightning like this, several factors are involved. You have to be in the right place at the right time. Being in or near a thunderstorm may be the right place, but if the sky conditions aren't dark enough, it won't work. You have to have enough proficiency with a camera to allow you to know how to set the lens open until a bolt of lightning strikes in front of you, then close it.

Maybe one of the major ingredients of lightning photography is patience. The camera covers only a small slice of the world before you. You have to be willing to wait out the perfect storm that dumps bolts out in front of you. And that may take several storms. So persistence may be the greatest factor. If you want to get what you're going for, you have to keep trying and not give up just because it doesn't fall into your lap. Knowing others have had success at the same quest helps you know it can be done. And it wasn't any easier for anybody else to do it.

Skill, patience, knowing what you want, persistence, and a little bit of luck, all goes into an "I'm a lucky dog" shot, as well as with most anything else in life worth having.

But remember, if you get struck by lightning, all of the above will seem trivial in comparison.

26

(27) Sciple's Mill is the last water-powered gristmill in Mississippi. Don's shot of it encompasses the scope of the building. On the left are the gates that hold back the water in the millpond. On the right is the mill itself. The water wheel is a turbine that is enclosed in a concrete box. You can see it on the right bank of Running Tiger Creek between the water gates and the mill itself.

Edward Sciple is the current proprietor. He is the fourth generation (or fifth?) of his family to run the mill. Edward always tells folks he was a TV repairman when his father passed the mill on to him. And he says he could make a hundred times more money repairing TVs. But he'd a hundred times rather grind corn.

If money is our definition of satisfaction and success, we could all become mighty sad and end up failures when the next recession hits. But if we've found something in life that gives us our purpose other than our bank accounts, then we'll still be smiling. And I hope we all have more sense than dollars, anyway.

28

(28) Adam Carr of Potts Camp is an early riser by the looks of his submission, "Morning Mist." This shot was taken at Bethlehem in Marshall County. Adam says simply:

— Adam: Morning mists are common in the red clay hills around Potts Camp.

— Walt: I wish Bethlehem there in Marshall County was big enough to have a post office. I'd drive all the way up there just to get my Christmas cards postmarked at Bethlehem. And maybe if I had that incentive, I'd actually get industrious enough to send out Christmas cards *every* year instead of every third or fourth year like we do now. And thank goodness for the twelve days of Christmas lasting on over into January so our still-up Christmas tree has a reason to be there.

27

And if our mornings where we live whispered day into existence like the morning in Adam's picture, maybe I'd get up early more often and greet it. But we are enjoying payback time now as we regularly sleep in until 6:30 or 7:00 every morning after years of having to get up early and do things like sign on radio stations or go to 7:00 a.m. classes. I'm not like my Aunt Ermie who told me that even though Uncle Lloyd had retired from TVA many years before, they still got up at five o'clock every morning without an alarm. If I got up at 5:00 a.m. it would *have* to be without an alarm. Because I sure wouldn't *set* one for that early!

29

However, Benny Gresham, one of the three brothers who operated WJPR radio in Greenville, told me at my first job in radio that people who could get themselves up early and get going in the morning were destined to become successful in life because so few other people could do so. Sounded like advice from the experience of someone who was older and wiser than I until I realized Benny was just trying to talk me into taking the sign-on shift.

Emily, our youngest granddaughter, used to have to spend the night at our house often when her mother Tammy's and her father Brad's shifts at the University of Mississippi emergency room and as a paramedic with a local ambulance service, respectively, overlapped. Emily has always amazed me with the things she comes up with every so often. For instance, one particularly foggy morning when Emily woke up and looked out the kitchen window as I fixed my coffee, she turned to me and wide-eyed asked, "Pops. What happened to the world?"

From the looks of the world on a morning like the one in the picture from Bethlehem Road in Marshall County, it seems to have softened up a bit overnight and looks a lot less threatening than it does on other days. That's a refreshing change from a blasting alarm clock and rude morning traffic. What happened to the world indeed!

(29) Here's another shot from Bethlehem Road in Marshall County taken by Adam Carr.

— Adam says of it: The spiderwort ought to be the official wildflower of Mississippi.

— Walt: I don't see why it can't be. As best I can tell by going to the Official Mississippi Web Site, the state doesn't even have an official wildflower. There is a state flower (Magnolia) and a state bird (Mockingbird) and even a state shell and a state rock—but no state wildflower. Start writing those letters.

(30) The next photo is also from Adam Carr. He calls it, "Along Callicutt Road." The location is Callicutt Road in Marshall County."

— Adam: A bygone view along Callicutt Road. The pasture and tree lines in the mid-range have been removed and improved for the sake of agricultural efficiency.

— Walt: This picture brings to mind another of those word mix-ups I grew up with in my Christian family: *pasture* and *pastor*. Usually context would make clear which was which. But when combined with trying to "feed the sheep" or "working with the flock," sometimes it could still be a bit fuzzy.

But a good pasture and a good pastor ought to leave you with a similar feeling of peace and serenity like this picture leaves you with.

(31) Adam Carr sent in another shot he calls "Boatner Road." Boatner Road is also in Marshall County. Adam's thoughts on the shot:

— Adam: Fall browns and new road gravel invite the walker to explore the countryside.

— Walt: I perk up at the name Boatner. That was my Daddy's middle name. I knew Boatner was a family name but didn't know much about it until my sister Ermie (named for the aunt) told me that years and years ago she worked at the *Delta Democrat-Times* in Greenville. And you know how folks in the Delta try to throw names around fishing for your pedigree or to show off theirs. Well, the Carters who ran the paper had come from Hammond, Louisiana. Hodding Carter III was at that time editor, and his uncle, John Boatner Carter, was in charge of the advertising department where Ermie worked. When it came up in a conversation that Daddy was a Louisiana boy and that his middle name was also Boatner, we had the advantage because Boatner had been my Daddy's great-grandmother Josephine Grayson's maiden name, whereas John Carter was only named for a family friend, Grandmother Josephine's nephew Judge John S. Boatner. Kin trumps friend any time in the South.

I like road pictures like this. The road before you is clear. Then it tops a hill in the far distance. And any number of possibilities lie on the other side of that hill, and most of those side roads, detours, and even dead-ends are completely up to you. But the farther you go down the road, the fewer and fewer places are left that the road will ultimately lead to. Don't let your kids get so far down their roads that they have limited their options by not getting things like a good education that will allow them to continue down the main road farther.

Someone told me something interesting about headstones. There is only one thing on our headstone that we have any control over. It's not our name or birth date or death date. But it's that little dash that separates the birth and death dates. And what we do during that dash is *totally* up to us.

30

31

32

(32) Marion Cospeclich Mills of Bay St. Louis calls the next picture, "Living Life on the Bayou." This is a pre-Camille photo taken on Joe's Bayou, which empties into Bay St. Louis. Marion says of the photo:

— Marion: A typical day of work for Alfred Cospelich's Shipyard and Marina, located on Joe's Bayou, before Hurricane Camille. The business of building and repairing wooden boats had been taught to Alfred by his father, Joseph Cospelich, who owned and operated the business since 1909. The bustling business was loved and enjoyed by generations of family growing up here. After the 1947 hurricane and then Camille, it was built back and business went on as usual.

Many fellow Mississippians and Louisiana fishermen and sportsmen knew the place well and did business here. When Alfred passed away in 1972, his wife, Allie Poillion Cospelich, ran the business along with the help and knowledge of her father and brothers until the early 1990s.

Since Katrina, the family has rebuilt their homes and still live along Joe's Bayou. The old shipyard is still there to help remember the times gone by and the love of life on "The Bayou."

(33) Here is a shot of what we raised mostly in Ms. Jo's flowerbed last year, wildlife. Well, I guess the lilacs actually did outnumber the lizards, thinking back on it. But the lizards were colorful and entertaining, especially when they did acrobatics across the amaryllis buds like this fellow.

33

34

(34) Cliff Hudson in Louisville calls the next picture, "Fall Colors Along an Old Woods Road in Winston County."

Here's another road that wanders into an unknown distance. You know where you are but not so much what's beyond that far turn. And there is a little more urgency in this picture because it is the fall of the year. And as we all grow toward the fall of our years, we tend to grow anxious about where the road is leading.

I'll tell you something Ms. Jo and I have tried to do. We try not to be overly concerned about what's coming up tomorrow, because by and large, you can't possibly know for sure what's ahead, anyway. And by like token, we've tried to quit agonizing over what has happened in the past. Unless some of Einstein's laws can be put into a working time machine, there is absolutely nothing that can be done about what has already happened, so why continue to fret with it? So what does that leave? Today. I don't mean we can worry and fret about today (I guess we could). But if we drop the past and the future, we have time to enjoy today. The past is gone, and the future will get here soon enough; deal with it then.

Look around at today. Just as in this picture, where we are at the moment ain't too bad. The leaves are beautiful, and it looks as if the temperature wouldn't be too uncomfortable. So why not enjoy where we are?

But I guess it's human nature to spend all our energy trying to look into a crystal ball to see what's ahead to the extent that we don't even know where we are right now. As far as anticipating what lies ahead around those blind curves of life, I think Mark Twain summed it up best when he said something to the gist of, he had "Lived a long life filled with problems. Fortunately, 90 percent of them never came to pass."

35

(35) The next picture is also by Cliff Hudson and he calls it "Control Burning in a Winston County Pine Plantation."

Smoke turns the sky yellow, and you can smell it. Get close enough, and you can feel the heat of the fire. If you are used to seeing the pictures of the big blazes in California on the evening newscast, then you may think what is happening in this picture is a disaster. Actually, it is anything but that. This is a disaster in the *un*-making.

Timber is Mississippi's number one agricultural product. I cringe when some ad on TV proclaims that their product "saves trees." They act as if people go out and cut down trees at random to make paper for hand towels and lumber for houses. Here in Mississippi, trees are raised just like cotton and soybeans. Someone may as well promote a product by proclaiming that it says saves cotton from being picked. I suppose maybe they are trying to say their product is environmentally friendly. But in Mississippi, trees are grown on purpose to be cut and used as wood products.

And that's not to say we are chopping down all our forests. We have more wooded acres in Mississippi today than we had a hundred years ago. And we'll have more next year than this because of practices like that pictured here, of protecting our woodlands.

Pines can take the heat. The scrub plants that grow beneath them and rob them of their food and then become hazards for real forest fires can't take the heat. So, the idea is to regularly set small fires to burn out the pest plants, and the end result is a healthy forest.

36

(36) Darlene Fryery Bane of Louisville snapped the next photo. She calls it "Weeds." And she says of it:

— Darlene: This is a patch of weeds in the ditch by my mailbox. A nuisance until I caught them in the right light and saw their beauty.

— Walt: What a hopeful thought. I suppose almost everyone has had a less than stellar self-image at some point. And I suppose we have always hoped that someone would come along and catch us in the right light and see our better "hidden" qualities that we know we have in us somewhere. And sometimes that does happen.

(37) The barn and the fence is another picture submitted by Darlene Fryery Bane. She titled it "Foggy September Morning." And she says:

— Darlene: I drive by the farm of the late Mr. and Mrs. Travis Triplett every day. It's a beautiful country scene.

— Walt: I am a big fan of old barns. They've lasted past their usefulness, most of them. And outlasted their builders, too. Now they are monuments to the past and to a different age. The fact that they still stand attests to how well they were constructed to begin with, and how central and important they were to the operation of the farm they served.

37

38

(38) Here's another photo by Darlene Fryery Bane of Louisville, "Fall Leaves on a Stained-Glass Sky."

— Darlene says: Taken on the Ole Miss campus. Every stage of life is beautiful.

— Walt: Hard to top that for commentary. Over the years of doing TV features in Mississippi, I have noticed that for a state not particularly known for its fall color, we have some beautiful leaves here in the autumn. But I think the reason we're not known for our colorful autumns is Mississippi doesn't have any mountains. And our tallest hilltops are less than a thousand feet above sea level. And even though the summit is that tall, the bases of those hills are only a couple of hundred feet below the top. So in perspective, they don't look all that tall.

Now on the other hand, states known for fall color, New England for example, have lots of hillsides where trees can show off en masse. And massive numbers of glowing trees spread out over a mountainside overhead unobstructed get noticed.

Now, if you walk through the woods in Mississippi in fall, we have just as many pretty trees, and just as much color here, if not more, than there. I'd put the reds, oranges, yellows, and purples of a sweet gum up against a New England maple any day. But you'll never see sweet gums splayed out over a hillside in Mississippi like you'll see the maples massed there. It's not that we don't have the sweet gums in substantial numbers. We've got gobs of them! We just don't have the hillsides where you can get the proper vantage to see them all at once.

So autumn color in Mississippi is more on an individual tree basis. It's there, but you may have to take a walk in a forest to really see the trees.

(39) David DeGuire of Brandon is the photographer of our next picture, titled "Reservoir Rainbow."

— David says: When I first moved to Mississippi (during the Flood of 1979), I was taught how quickly Mother Nature could change the weather, and this photo reflects a quickly moving rainstorm. I took this photo in September 2009. Rain over Madison County and the setting sun produced a beautiful double rainbow over the reservoir!

— Walt: Southwest Airlines should buy this shot for use in their ads!

39

40

(40) Speaking of photos taken out of airplane windows, this next shot is one I took while we were flying over either Arizona or New Mexico on the way to Dallas from Los Angeles in 2009.

When I fly, I usually have a camera handy, too. There is always something interesting down below, especially over places I don't get to see that often. I am always intrigued by the look of the mountains and deserts out West. In this shot, down below is the parched earth, yet it has obviously been washed by lots of water. It looks like it drains into a Mississippi River mud flat, only bigger—and drier.

41

42

I have to wonder if all those watermarks come from just the occasional rains that fall here today. Or are these the trails left from an era when this area used to be a lot wetter? Whichever, it obviously took a lot of time to make all those water trails. But what does the earth have if not lots of time?

(41) Deonna Carroll submitted this photograph. She calls it "Father of the Year." Here's what she says about it.

— Deonna: Long Beach, Mississippi, 2009—Mardi Gras party on my slab on Third Street. I was standing in the back of a truck away from the crowds. I looked through my zoom lens and watched this man for hours. I was amazed as he carried both little girls and still found the occasional free hand to catch beads. Here in the South we start giving gifts in December and don't stop until spring!

— Walt: What a daddy won't do for a child! I also like the Mardi Gras parades on the coast. The coast parades are for families. Matter of fact, *all* the Mississippi parades are family oriented; from Natchez to D'lo, it is seen to that the kids get the beads.

(42) Here's another picture Deonna Carroll sent us from the coast. These are, according to her title, "Roseate Spoonbills in Long Beach Harbor." They are a rarity in Mississippi. Nice shot! (See "Lucky Dog" implications a few pictures back.)

— Deonna says of her find: Even though I no longer live on the beach, I still like to take my breakfast down to the harbor and watch the birds. This morning the tide was out, and I noticed something pink. I quickly drove over and found this mated pair of birds. One of the birds had an injured leg and was hopping around. The mate stayed close by as they fed in the shallow waters. I informed the Harbor Master and the Department of Wildlife to make them aware of these rare sights. Everyone was excited. I was not able to make it back the next day. A few days later when I returned, they were gone. From Bay St. Louis to Gulfport, by far the Long Beach harbor has the most wildlife. You never know what you will find.

— Walt: I looked up the roseate spoonbill on that clearinghouse of all reference materials, Google (mainly at Deonna's insistence to check her spelling of "roseate," not a word you use every day) and found that this particular bird is often misidentified as a flamingo because of its pink color. But everybody knows that flamingos are only found in yards. Well, that's the only place I have ever seen them, except in the zoo.

The several references that were instantly put at my fingertips also did not list Mississippi as one of this particular spoonbill's habitats. In the Northern/Western

43

Hemisphere they are found in Florida (480 breeding pair) and Texas. Some in Louisiana, maybe.

But a map highlighted the whole Amazon basin as natural habitat in South America. No doubt they number a "Brazillion" or more there. (From the George Bush, Jr., joke where he sees in the morning headlines that thirteen Brazilian soldiers were injured in an ambush and he asks an aide, "How many is a Brazilian?")

Our really rare bird that they want to catch still alive probably went extinct sixty or seventy years ago: the ivory-billed woodpecker. They outnumbered Cajuns in the south Mississippi and Louisiana swamps. But the cutting of old growth timber decreased their habitat to the point that most agree they are no longer among us.

Still, studies are funded to put microphones in the deep swamps to try to detect their unique call. And a few years ago, someone in a swamp in Arkansas (please!) shot about fifteen frames of video of what looked to me like a great blue heron flying past them out of focus and tried to pass it off as an ivory-billed woodpecker. Well, the camera shot was so shaky that you can't prove it wasn't.

Most likely the ivory-billed woodpecker passed the way of the dodo bird and the nickel Coke long ago. We still have examples of each, but no live survivors. But still, every time I am near a swamp with my camera, I keep a sharp eye out for an ivory-billed woodpecker. For one thing, I hope they have actually survived against all odds. That would give me hope for our culture. And for another, an actual photo of an ivory-billed woodpecker alive today ought to be worth, oh what, about a brazillion dollars?

(43) Deonna Carroll gets around as much as I do. In this photograph she moves us from the coast inland to one of my favorite haunts, the Natchez City Cemetery. Her title for this photo is "Weeping Angel of Natchez, Mississippi."

And she says of her work. My husband and I love history. I spend a great deal of time in cemeteries for the history and the incredible artwork. People often say that they would not go to a cemetery alone. I laugh and say, "The dead don't mind visitors. They never seem to complain to me." During this trip I had my husband Larry Carroll with me celebrating our anniversary. He is very patient with me as we travel and take pictures. The attention to detail of cemetery ironwork is fascinating to me. I love iron and the permanence of it—until it is hit by salt water.

— Walt: One of my favorite haunts, Natchez City Cemetery! I shot a picture of this *exact* wrought iron gate in the Natchez City Cemetery to use as an example of the kinds of gates that had been stolen from the cemetery in Rodney (Mississippi River ghost town halfway between Natchez and Vicksburg, shade a few miles in Natchez's favor) in a recent *Look Around Mississippi* story for WLBT.

Now, from there we could go on to Eudora Welty's cemetery photographs, which included Rodney, and mention that, while I have found many of the graveyards she documented in her photography, I haven't found them all, but I am still looking.

Or, I could make mention of my religious upbringing again and my confusion with similar sounding words, such as cemetery and seminary. Finally got a handle on that one. If the fellow was going to preach in our church the next Sunday, then odds were he wasn't in a cemetery but probably was attending a seminary. Some rebellious evangelists of today equate the two. (They probably have attended few of either.)

Our good friend in Natchez, Don Estes, who was the director of the Natchez City Cemetery for years, has a wonderful book he's written about the cemetery, *Legends of the Natchez City Cemetery*. Everything I could say about the cemetery is in Don's book. Go buy one.

And when Natchez's world-famous mystery writer Greg Iles set the opening of his latest book, *The Devil's Punchbowl*, in Natchez City Cemetery at midnight, I knew I was going to like the book no matter what else followed after that.

It was funny. We have a group of us who attended Greenville High about the same time, and we go out to eat and occasionally take an excursion together. Recently, all went to Natchez for a weekend getaway. It was great! Our friend Karlyn Ritchie, manager of

Rosalie, gave us a great private tour of that beautiful old home. We ate fried chicken at Carriage House Restaurant, which actually was the carriage house at one time, at the stately old home Stanton Hall. And we even took a tour of my favorite house in Natchez, Longwood; the home was left unfinished because when the War Between the States broke out, the northern artisans from Philadelphia, Pennsylvania, who were working on it dropped their tools and fled home. And 160 years later those tools are still where they were dropped.

As our little group was eating at Mammy's Cupboard the next day, someone came in and told us that Greg Iles was having an advance book signing at Trinity Episcopal School, which is just a few miles up Highway 61 from where we were eating. We would drive right past it on the way back into Natchez.

So on the way back into town we stopped by to buy a copy of the book and get Greg to sign it. *But*! They were completely sold out of books by the time we got there. *However*! The librarian, saying she had several reserve copies, more than enough for our little group, allowed any of us who wanted to, to purchase one of her copies to get it signed while Greg was there.

I apologized for taking all her books before she had had time to read a copy herself. In a whisper she confided to me, "Oh I just love his books, but I can't read them!" Too much graphic language for a librarian. She'd be "shushing" the whole time she was reading!

(44) While we are in Natchez City Cemetery, this is one of my photographs. It is of the Irene Ford grave. Irene was about ten years old when she died in 1871. A set of concrete steps was sunk behind her headstone to the coffin level where a windowpane was set into a concrete wall so the little glass coffin could be seen inside the grave. The story goes that little Irene was terribly afraid of storms. And every time a thunderstorm came up, her mother would go to the cemetery and descend the steps and sit with her until the storm passed.

Jo and I were in Natchez on a flying trip to no doubt try to accomplish several tasks, one of which was to shoot the breaks that would be edited between the stories in an upcoming *Look Around Mississippi* TV show.

I was about chest deep down the steps at Irene Ford's grave delivering lines into the camera up above when the camera battery went dead. That was almost the last straw in a straw-strewn trip. Jo, realizing my exasperation, told me not to move. She would go back to the vehicle and get another battery. As Jo was jogging to the equipment bag, I just sighed out, "This is *frustrating*!"

Then, a little voice, not audible, but I heard it in my brain, from below me to my left, about coffin level, answered, "You think *you're* frustrated!"

Needless to say I was startled. But then I got to thinking, ya' know, so far as we can tell for sure, the only time in all of space and time that we are able to interact with creation is right now while we are alive and in our bodies. I can pick flowers, do dishes, and fetch batteries. And if I am frustrated over something, right now I have the ability to do something about it.

So I quit complaining and was suddenly awfully thankful to be alive.

45

(45) Joan Easterling Nicholson of Mount Olive sent in the next picture. She calls it "Church Window."

— Joan says: This church is down the road from my home. I have always been fascinated by it because of its charm. It was founded in 1830 and glimmers with beauty. This particular photo captures the early morning sun through one of the church windows. To me this reflects the innocence of the early morning and the peacefulness of rural Mississippi.

— Walt: There was a time not all that long ago that people, especially country people, loved to go to church on Sunday, because it was about the only time neighbors got to see one another. Even into my college years while I was pastor of little Good Hope Baptist Church in northern Madison County, almost on the Attala County line, most of the old folks still associated Sunday services with the chance to catch up on the community.

When I tell people the name of my little church, folks say they know where it is. But I quickly tell them, "No. It's not that Good Hope." Good Hope is the most common name for a church or a community or a community that grew up around a church in Mississippi.

That was another lifetime altogether. But the picture of the church window reminds me a lot of those days. The annual revival capped off with homecoming and dinner on the grounds. The annual community Thanksgiving service that rotated among our church and Shiloh Presbyterian, then Shrock Methodist and Seniash Methodist.

Being a student pastor had a lot of pluses. The extra income was always welcome. Learning the discipline of having to prepare a sermon a week in addition to everything else that was going on helped me get a handle on how busy life would be from then on. But what we especially liked was a real home-cooked meal at least once a week for Sunday dinner.

One of the old couples who were still living when we were serving at Good Hope, Brewer and Robbie Lee Browning, even had what they called a preacher's room up at the front of their house. It was an extra little bedroom with a little sitting room attached that Brewer built when he built the house. We spent many Saturday nights before Easter Sunday there. Talk about cold! It seems the Easter cold snap always hit the night we'd sleep in that country bedroom with no heat. And our feet would stick to the floor the next morning when we first stepped out of bed!

They had a wood heater in their living room. I remember Robbie Lee telling me how much company the crackling fire in that heater was to her on cold winter days when Brewer wasn't at home. Brewer and Robbie Lee are gone now. But I'll never forget them and the easygoing country life they had and shared with us.

Good Hope Church has actually grown significantly since I was there. They've had running water for a long time, now, which we didn't have during my stay there. They've even built a big fellowship center.

I got a call from the *Madison County Herald* newspaper when Good Hope dedicated their new fellowship hall. They were asking me as a former pastor to give them a comment about Good Hope's expansion. I was, of course, delighted for the church. But I told the reporter that we had had a building program while I was pastor there, also. A significant one, too. We replaced the old outhouse with a brand-new two-holer!

(46) Speaking of old times, this next photograph is dated from 1910. And "dated" is accurate because it is a picture printed on a postcard, and the postmark on back is dated that year. Ellen B. Bigbie from Laurel sent it in. In the picture we meet the Taylors in Ellisville.

— Ellen says: This is Camilla Taylor Bynum, Richard Jobe Taylor, and Nancy Jane Reynolds Taylor in Ellisville, Mississippi. This picture is the reverse of a postcard that was mailed to Jobe and Nancy's daughter in about 1910. Jobe and Nancy Jane are my great-great-grandparents. This is one of my favorite old family photos because not only does it show the house in Ellisville, but the letter on the back gives a little peek into their lives.

46

R. J. Taylor served in the War Between the States and came home and was elected surveyor for Newton County. He taught school for fifty years in Newton and Jones Counties, often serving as a boarding-out teacher in the outer reaches of the county while his family lived in Ellisville. One particular school he served was in the Erata community northeast of Laurel.

— Walt: Ellen obviously has the same love for old photographs that I mentioned early on in this book that I have. What better way to let you know that you are just the latest page in a family book whose chapters go way back than to be able to look into the faces of those who came before you.

(47) Carolyn R. Forbes of Foxworth sent in this picture of a bottle tree in the snow. I think a major significance of this photo is where it was taken, in Carolyn's yard in Foxworth on a snowy day. She says Toby J. Martin made the bottle tree.

A snowy day in Foxworth? Man! That's a long way down in the southern part of the state for it to be snowing.

My sister Linda, in Huntsville, Alabama, as well as a cousin, Susan Moss in Atlanta, both commented to me that this has been an unusual winter (2009–2010) for snow in the South where they live. More snows and bigger snows than they've seen in a while.

Here's another family story. One day when my Mama's brother Greyson Cummings was a youngster, he went to work at the sawmill with Granddaddy one balmy spring morning. By dinnertime it had clouded up and turned blustery. And by the time they started home from the sawmill that afternoon it was snowing. Uncle Greyson had to hang onto the wagon and run behind it to stay warm because he had no coat with him. Modern-day forecasters would have warned us of the cold snap days in advance. But would have taken the adventure out of it in doing so.

47

(48) The next photo comes from Cecilia Ann Harris Gossman of Diamondhead. It's another old family photograph.

— Cecilia said of it: Each summer the children from Palmer Home for Children in Columbus, Mississippi, would have a picnic in Lee Park. I remember drinking water from the artesian well. Notice that no one has on shoes. Yes, we did own shoes, but we could hardly wait until summer time to go barefooted! Evelyn Williams, later to be Evelyn Williams McPhail, is second from right, and many years later she became the co-chairman of the Republican National Committee. The chairman at the time was Haley Barbour. The picture was taken in the 1940s.

— Walt: Nothing says summer in Mississippi like watermelon, crape myrtles, and going barefooted. I don't know if kids go barefooted today like we used to. And I can't really remember why we did it, for that matter.

But when school was out for the summer, the shoes came off. Can you remember the feel of mud between your toes and the feel of wet grass and how rocks were so uncomfortable at the beginning of summer, but by the end of summer you could run across a gravel road without a thought?

Someone told me that their daddy wouldn't let them go barefooted until it got warm enough for the folks bank fishing to sit with their bottoms on the ground instead of on their bait buckets.

48

The little stickers that grow in yards were always a problem for barefooters. And when we boys in the neighborhood got on a daring streak, sooner or later someone would dare someone else to walk barefooted across Mrs. Hammock's yard. It was *loaded* with stickers and we all knew it.

I remember cutting my toe with one of Mama's paring knives while playing a game of stretch barefooted. I don't really remember the object of the game; tossing a knife and sticking it in the ground close enough for you to stretch one foot to it while not moving the other, but far enough so your opponent couldn't do so without falling over is the way it worked, I think: a crude version of Twister using sharp objects.

And if you didn't get your first tetanus shot because you stepped on a fishhook while barefooted, then you missed a rite of passage in childhood.

49

(49) Clyde E. Gousset of Natchez has sent us a piece of history.

— Clyde says of the photo: These are two of the remaining four columns that were once part of the Forest Plantation home owned by my great-great-grandfather, Sir William Dunbar.

The two columns pictured are the only ones that are still full length. The other two are broken off at the second story. The house burned in 1851 and was never rebuilt. It's said to have burned on Christmas Eve. William Dunbar was an inventor, scientist, and explorer. Along with George Hunter, he explored the lower part of the Louisiana Purchase in 1804 for President Thomas Jefferson, from Natchez, Mississippi, to Hot Springs, Arkansas, by way of the Mississippi, Black, and Ouachita Rivers. A documentary film titled *The Forgotten Expedition* was funded and produced by a grant from Ouachita Baptist University about the expedition. Dunbar's original trip journal, compass, and other papers are on loan to the university at this time. Dunbar died October 16, 1810, at the age of sixty-two.

— Walt: Our daughter Tammy was texting me this very evening looking for suggestions of famous Mississippians for a fourth-grade assignment for our youngest granddaughter, Emily. I sent her Jefferson Davis, Elvis, and William Faulkner, as well as Tennessee Williams (Mississippi Williams wouldn't have flowed as easily), Eudora Welty, and some others.

I nearly sent her William Dunbar's name, but so few people have ever heard of him I didn't know if he would help or hurt Emily's grade. I probably wouldn't know anything about him myself had it not been for a video presentation on the colonial history of Mississippi I wrote and produced many years ago for the Colonial Dames. In colonial days, Dunbar was one of the outstanding Mississippians.

One monument to Dunbar is still here today. Back when the United States took over a great deal of West Florida from Spain (that area that included the Natchez District),

President Washington commissioned Andrew Ellicott to survey the thirty-first parallel, which was the border between the United States and what was left of Spanish territory.

Spain hired Sir William Dunbar to be their surveyor and check behind Ellicott. According to Dunbar, Ellicott placed the line about a hundred yards too far to the north. However, considering they were using crude survey instruments and sighting by the constellations to get their bearings, I'm amazed they could plot the line at all! I don't know that I could have placed it on the correct continent, much less only a hundred yards off!

But the line they surveyed and finally agreed on still lives with us today as the state line between Mississippi and Louisiana south of Woodville, between Woodville and St. Francisville, Louisiana. It starts at the Mississippi River south of Fort Adams and runs eastward to the Pearl River.

(50) Cindy Gustafson of Southaven took this next shot. She calls it "The End of the Day," and simply says of it that it was taken at Arkabutla Lake, Hernando Point.

A friend of mine says when they'd come back off vacation, his daddy would have snapped a picture of every sunset. If they looked anything like this one, can you blame him?

50

51

(51) This is another of Cindy's photos. She calls this one "Rising from the Fog." She says this one was taken at Enid, Mississippi, at George Payne Cossar State Park.

Fog at daybreak commands reverence and contemplation. You speak in hushed tones. You think quiet thoughts. The fog shuts out the rest of the world, thereby automatically reducing your sphere of attention to just what's closest to you. Maybe you can hear yourself think in a situation like that. Maybe you can even hear God whispering. If nothing else, maybe you don't have to hear everything else that demands your attention elsewhere. At least you can ignore it until the fog starts to burn off and the volume turns up once again.

(52) Cindy Gustafson shifts gears from colorful sunsets and muted sunrises to the vibrant colors of a friend's lake in Southaven, Mississippi. Norman Winter invited me to conduct some seminars at the Garden and Patio shows this year. I am no gardener. I haven't been all that successful at raising much of anything since I used to plant radishes when I was a kid. They always did really well. I only wish I had liked radishes.

However, just because I know very little about the subtleties of horticulture, I still put on an important seminar because I know the most important element in having a great patch of vegetables or a beautiful bed of flowers or a yard and lake like the one in this picture. The most important element to have any of that (and lots more of the best things on life) is time.

Applied time is the only way we get anything in life. Life is lived at the speed of time. In some respects time just crawls, like a kid waiting for Christmas. In other ways it flies, like an adult trying to hold *back* Christmas. But in either case, it passes. But while it is passing, we need to put it to use. Start today doing whatever it is that in six months you'll be wishing you had started six months ago.

(Hint: It's the same thing you are *currently* wishing you had started six months *back*. Then, six months from now, you will have started doing it six months ago and won't just be wishing about it anymore.)

(53) Hank Lamb of Greenwood sends the photo of what he titled "The Sunset Depot." The old depot is in Sunflower, Mississippi, in the Delta. Hank says the depot was moved

to this field from another location. There are no railroad tracks anywhere near it.

This picture is sort of like two sunsets in one; the actual rays of the setting sun at the end of the day and the symbolic sun that has set on the era of railroading from which this depot came.

When this depot was new, choo choo trains really went "choo choo" because they were steam driven. The little train that said, "I think I can, I think I can," building in rhythm as it picked up steam, couldn't have said those words with the same effect in this day of the whir of diesel electric engines. Also, there would have been little question of whether the engine could make it or not make it as a diesel. A modern engine most likely could.

52

Old depots fall in a similar category as old barns, no longer as necessary as they once were, but too important to our past and to the memory of the building of our society to ignore them and not treat them with respect. And it's nice someone thought enough of this one to save it.

53

54

(54) Benjamin Hart was a little ways away from his home in Pascagoula when he was taken by a view that stops many travelers in Natchez. His photo was snapped from the top of Silver Street where the street slips off the bluff to Natchez Under the Hill below, giving a grand view of the Highway 84 bridges, and offering a spectacular place to watch the sun sinking into Louisiana beyond the bridges at day's end.

Benjamin calls his shot "Sunset on the Mississippi, Natchez, Mississippi." He says it was a sort of accidental picture that won him a blue ribbon in the Jackson County Fair.

Wasn't it Oprah who said she gets the luckiest when she prepares the hardest? When you get the best camera you can afford and then practice with it and learn how to use it well enough so you know when the auto function is not going to give you the kind of results you want, and have fiddled with it enough to know what to do to get those results and then find yourself standing at the right place with camera in hand and a wonderful photograph unfolding before you, and you lift the viewfinder and calculate the composition and exposure and then click the shutter and get the shot, then you are Oprah's kind of lucky.

(55) Doug Herbert, Jr., who lives in Arlington, Virginia, sent in the next photo. He calls it "Furrows & Delta Church." He says he's not sure of the exact location, but it's out in the country near Louise in Humphreys County on Highway 149.

— Doug says of the picture: When I was a kid, my parents lived down in south Mississippi (Foxworth), and it seemed like we would constantly be driving up to Greenwood from Carrollton to visit relatives. I was convinced the Delta was the most boring and ugliest place in the world, with no redeeming features whatsoever. In a desperate attempt to amuse myself, I would put my chin down on the backseat window (rolled down, no AC, of course) and make myself dizzy watching the various optical illusions of cotton rows flashing by the little two-lane roads.

Now, when my wife and I return to Mississippi and drive up to Greenville to see her family, I find the Delta an endlessly fascinating subject for photography, which my twelve-year-old self would have been horrified to learn about. This photo was my effort to recapture some of the feel of that poor little boy playing optical games watching cotton furrows from the family car.

— Walt: I know the kinds of optical illusions Doug is referring to. Plowed rows come to a singular point out toward the horizon if the field is long enough, sort of like the

55

56 57

universe is supposed to have originated from a singularity at the big bang and then has expanded outward ever since. And riding past the rows up close, they dance into and out of your field of vision while the far point seems to follow you like the moon follows you at night.

We were coming back home to Greenville from a visit to Fulton when I was a boy, and as I let my eyes go out of focus on the passing cornfield to the side of us. It looked like people were running through it, elbows and knees pumping high, keeping up with the car.

My favorite optical illusion was actually a mirage, I guess: the water in the road ahead that evaporates by the time you get to it. From a distance back, it looks too deep to drive through. But by the time the car gets to where you had seen it, the road is dry, only to have the mirage reform up ahead a way. Sometimes Daddy would play along with my pretend cries of warning of the impending danger from the flooded road. Sometimes he wouldn't. Depended on how his day was going, I guess.

Driving, I don't get to see any of the side view optical illusions anymore. And none of the kids seemed to want to play "flood" with the mirage in the road ahead as I did when I was young. Too smart for all of that. I suppose they think I'm crazy for trying to convince them it was water. I wasn't trying to convince them the mirage was really water so much as I was trying to convince them to be children while they were still young enough to be.

(56) Kevin Hudson of Louisville sent in the next series of photos. The first of his set is of the Church of the Redeemer in Biloxi as it looked after Camille but before Katrina. It survived Camille, but Katrina proved who was boss.

Jefferson Davis was a member of the Church of the Redeemer in his later years, although he never worshiped in the building destroyed by Camille. Davis died in 1889. The building was built in 1891.

We marveled at a storm so powerful it could rip apart such an impressive building. Then came Katrina and demolished what had been left by Camille. Our appreciation of powerful storms was appropriately upgraded.

(57) Kevin's next photograph is of "Fog on the Pearl." This shot was made near Philadelphia, Mississippi.

No matter what Sweet Potato Queen Jill Conner Brown says about "less being more" not even making sense, here is a case where less actually is more. The barest of detail in the foreground and even the lack of color makes this photo a stronger interpretation of the scene than actually standing there in person looking at it would have been. My favorite photographer, Ansel Adams, regarded the photographic negative as the orchestral score, the photographer as the conductor of the orchestra, and the finished print as a symphony. The

58

59

final photo was therefore an interpretation of the negative (hence an interpretation of the scene photographed) and not a strict rendition.

(58) In the next photo, Kevin gives us a photograph of two of Mississippi's givens; the Mississippi River and kudzu. Kevin likes the way kudzu frames the bridges as the bridges reach toward Louisiana and the kudzu reaches toward the bridges.

Back when they introduced kudzu to the southland in the late 1920s or so, to be planted on newly cut highway road banks through the hills to help stabilize the soil against erosion, my Aunt Coleen, who is a plant lover and was still living at home at the time, came home with one of the kudzu plants from somewhere and set it out in the yard. When after only a few weeks the vine had grown all the way underneath the house from one end and had come out the other, Granddaddy made her dig it up and kill it.

That, to my knowledge, is the only kudzu plant to have ever been successfully killed in the South. All the rest are still alive and well and engulfing small towns even as you read this.

(59) Signs of the times. That isn't Kevin's title for this photograph, it's what comes to my mind when I see it. Kevin Hudson calls it "Law Office" and says its location is in his

hometown of Louisville. He says it is a sign from the past and tells us something of this building's history.

I suppose in most downtowns, especially in towns not considered big cities, the retail stores were located on the street level, but the floors overhead were rented out as offices. Dentists and doctors and accountants had offices up there, as well as lawyers. When the shopping centers kidnapped the downtown stores, those upper floor clients moved away, too, to small flat-roofed offices in the suburbs, leaving souvenirs of bygone days written on the windows left behind.

(60) Kevin's next shot is of one of the old inns on the Natchez Trace. There used to be one of these establishments about every twenty miles in the days when the Trace was in use. This is the only one still standing. It is maintained by the National Park Service.

60

61

Kevin titles his photo "Mount Locust," which is the name of the inn and the name on the Trace sign where it is located.

— Kevin says: Begun in 1780, Mount Locust still welcomes visitors along the Natchez Trace today.

— Walt: Granddaughter Taylor and I had an adventure at Mt. Locust one time. Back when I was writing the very first *Looking Around Mississippi* with Walt Grayson book, I had about a week to get everything finalized and sent to the publisher. The only thing I needed was a picture of the wood-framed Baptist church building in Rodney. I had lots of shots of the other church building there, the Presbyterian Church—the one with the cannonball still lodged in the front from a shelling it took from a Union gunboat in the Civil War. But I had mentioned the other church building in the text and wanted to put a picture of it in the book also.

(61) This is the Rodney Presbyterian Church that I already had many shots of.

(62) This is the Baptist Church in Rodney that I needed to quickly go take a picture of to send in to the publisher before the deadline.

62

So with just a few days left, one Sunday after church I asked Jo if she wanted to drive down to Rodney with me so I could snap that one remaining photograph. Jo flinched as if I had asked her to ride to Rodney or something, because Rodney is not exactly a pleasure trip from our house. Little of the roadway is four-lane. And once you get into the bluffs beyond Lorman, it's questionable whether you are even driving on pavement.

But granddaughter Taylor was spending the weekend with us, and Taylor's middle name is "Go!" So by the time I had asked Jo, "Do you want to go . . ." I heard the car door slam with Taylor already inside. So Taylor and I rode to Rodney. By the time I got there, I was beginning to feel the aftereffects of having eaten my own greasy cooking for breakfast that morning and I thought to myself that I was in a precarious place to potentially need a restroom. Then about that time Taylor blurted out, "Hey, Pops. I have to go to the bathroom." I tried to 'splain to her where we were. I told her this was Rodney, Mississippi, and the only restrooms here had leaves on them and you just go out behind them.

"But," I said, "If you and I can just use some self-restraint, we can head down this gravel road about five miles until it "T's" into an asphalt road, and then take a left on that road under the Natchez Trace to Highway 553, then turn right and go back to the Trace, then turn south on the Trace for two miles. There is a restroom right there at Coles Creek." Taylor explained that I obviously had no idea how badly she needed to go because I was giving her a lesson in geography when we really needed to be driving.

So we scampered down our five miles and turned left at the asphalt and right on 553 and south on the Trace and got to Coles Creek and discovered no fewer than about 250 people having a cookout and family reunion. And the lines to the men's and women's rooms looked a lot longer than Taylor and I could invest in at the time.

But I told her, "We are in luck! Because in the entire 444-mile stretch of the Natchez Trace there is only one place where restrooms are only two miles apart, and this is that place!" Two miles farther south from Coles Creek is Mt. Locust. However, the restroom at Mt. Locust is not on one of those horseshoe zip-ins like you find on the rest of the Trace. There, it is in a building at the back of the parking lot, about a quarter mile off the road. And the women's room is the farthest door from the front of the building.

I had my hand on the men's room door handle singing my ninth chorus of, "Thank You Jesus," when Taylor opened the women's room door and said, "It's dark in there. I don't want to go in by myself." I chose very short words to try to explain why right now wasn't a good time for me to discuss *anything*. But she was insistent. "It's scary in there, Pops. I don't want to go in there alone!"

I peeped in the door just to show her that there were no booger bears in there when I spied two stalls. "You take the back one and I'll take the front one," I told her.

And when Taylor finished up before I did, she opened the door wide and yelled to all the bears in the woods, "Hey, my Pops is in the women's room!"

Well, when we finished up, we walked on over to the restored inn to get some pictures. Ranger Chamberlain (whose family had owned the "stand" as it was called, and who was born there) was trying to get me to take a close up picture of a rattlesnake that had entwined itself through a split rail fence sunning itself. "Get on up there close on him, Walt. He can't bite you. He's not coiled up, so he can't strike." So I simply handed the ranger my camera and told him, "Suppose you show me exactly how close you think I ought to get."

63

(63) This is the photo of the rattlesnake entwined in the split rail fence. I honestly can't remember who snapped the shot, me or Ranger Chamberlain, or it might have even been Taylor.

Then, just as Taylor and I were walking back to the parking lot, my cell phone rang. The lady on the other end said I didn't know her, but she got my number from the front of my pocket calendar. She explained that they lived in Natchez and had just stopped at Mt. Locust and her granddaughter had found my calendar . . . on the floor of the women's room!

I tried to remain calm. So calm that perhaps the lady might have thought I just *kept* my calendar there. So after she told me what type car they were in and I told her what we were in and they said they would turn around and come back toward Mt. Locust and I told her that we'd start toward Natchez and meet in the middle somewhere, I calmly hung up my phone, calmly reached over and grabbed Taylor by the throat and calmly pulled her into my face and calmly told her, "I don't care what you tell them. But you convince them that *you* take my pocket calendar to the restroom with *you, all the time*!"

Instantly, the line Rodney Dangerfield turns and tells someone in Caddyshack (and I don't even remember the situation) came to mind. He said, "Now you know why tigers eat their young."

(64) Kevin Hudson has another of his renderings for us that he calls "Near the Cross." Kevin says it is a view from inside the rustic Sardis Church of a cross that stands in the churchyard. This particular Sardis Church is in Winston County.

I love the look and feel and smell of old churches. This building reminds me of the old Airmount Church in Yalobusha County. I did a story about a Sacred Harp singing at Airmount many, many years ago. Gordon Cotton, retired curator of the Old Courthouse Museum in Vicksburg, was there, and told me the setting at Airmount was just about perfect for an old timey singing. He said first of all, the songs *had* to be sung a cappella for it to be authentic. And the singing really needed to be in an old building like this. Then he told me to go out back to about the middle of the cemetery and listen. From there, the songs carried a bagpipe feel to them.

Old Airmount Church was set on fire by a fellow who got mad at his girlfriend, and it burned completely to the ground. I suppose he made his point. I'm sure the girlfriend was impressed and wanted him back immediately.

64

65

(65) Kevin's next photo he calls "Old Friends." The setting is in Montpelier, Mississippi, and Kevin says of it, "Two chairs invite you to sit for a while on the porch of the post office in Montpelier."

I recall my grandmother's home in Fulton had two swings on the front porch, not counting the chairs and a stool my grandfather made from a huge burl that had grown on a poplar tree. And Grandmother and the family actually had time to sit there. I have two swings on my porch, too. Mostly, my swings are just monuments to a memory from my childhood. I guess the biggest "old friend" this generation has lost is the ability to take time to relax.

66

(66) Kevin calls this one "Old Schoolhouse." He says this is the old Salem School where his grandfather graduated from high school in 1931. The school is in Noxubee County.

It's amazing these old places are still standing. But from the looks of the door, the building is obviously no longer used, except to bring back memories to those who attended there, or memories of those who attended there to younger generations who didn't.

(67) Kevin Hudson calls this next photo "Preparation." Travelers are warned to make preparations for the Judgment Day. The sign and the crosses are near Grenada, Mississippi.

I've seen whole fencerows covered in religious warning signs. (See photo 68.) If you tried to read them all while driving by, you'd meet your Maker real soon because of the wreck you'd be bound to have. You see things like that, and you might get a fleeting thought that someone who is slightly off kilter put it there. And you might smile to yourself. But then again, Noah was the first person to tell folks there was a day of reckoning coming. And he built a big boat in his yard as a sign of it. People thought he was a little touched. But according to the story, all of our DNA can be traced back to Noah. So don't be too quick to smirk. Obviously that sort of thing runs in our family.

JESUS
! 2
GOD
I TIM 3 16
JESUS
IS THE
FATHER
JO 14:9
JESUS
SAID
I AND MY
FATHER
ARE ONE
JO 10 30
THE FOXES HAVE
HOLES THE BIRDS
HAVE NEST MATT 8:20
REMEMBER LOTS
JESUS
SAID BE YE
PERFECT
MATT 5:48
THE WAGES
OF SIN IS
DEATH
QUIT WHILE
YOU CAN
HELL
IS
NEVER
FULL
AWAKE
TO
RIGHTEOUSNESS
AND
SIN NOT
WE ARE
SEED
SOWERS
I AND MY
FATHER ARE
ONE
JOHN 10:30
JOHN 14:9

68

Mis

67

(69) The last of Kevin Hudson's pictures is from Louisville. Kevin has titled it, appropriately, "Welcome to Our City." This is on a bench in downtown Louisville.

A town that goes to all the trouble to put out the bench to begin with and then paint on a welcome sign, makes you think they mean it. Thanks, Louisville.

69

(70) Joan Easterling Nicholson of Mount Olive gives us our next photograph. She calls it "Feeding Time."

— Joan says of it: Each afternoon (on our farm) is spent tending to the animals we have. This particular afternoon, camera in hand, I was able to capture the true essence of feeding time on our farm. This photo is of our registered Angus cattle heading past the pond and barn to the feeding trough.

— Walt: With raised hooves, this doesn't look like a leisurely stroll, either. My uncle had a dairy in Greenville when we were growing up. I would be standing on the levee after school looking out across the pastures in the late afternoon and see his pickup truck drive up to the barn in the distance. All the cows grazing on the side of the levee would lift their heads and start walking in the direction of the barn. They knew by the look and sound of his truck that it was feeding time.

I thought at the time that the cows were well trained, knowing it was time to eat when his truck drove up. Thinking back, maybe it was the other way around. Maybe they had him trained to drive up about the time they got hungry. And to make a lot of noise with his truck so they'd know when to expect their food.

70

(71) The next three photos come from John A. McDonald of Picayune. John titled the first of his photos of a bayou sunset "Calico Dreams."

— John says: I drove Menge Avenue from I-10 down to Long Beach, where I worked. On the west side of the road, there is a small bayou leading to the Wolf River. This bayou (I don't know if it is named) was the scene of many memorable sunsets at the end of the workday. It was always relaxing to stop and enjoy a great sunset, even with traffic whizzing by fifteen feet away.

— Walt: It is amazing that sometimes you are the only one who seems to see something like a sunset while the rest of the world rushes by with their heads down. You wonder if they just didn't notice, or maybe you missed something that everybody else knew about

71

that was more important than the sunset. I suspect it is that nobody else notices, or takes the time to stop and look. I guess when we figure that *every* day ends in a sunset, there will always be time to stop for the next one.

Kind of like as your kids are growing up, we feel they'll still be here tomorrow if we don't have time to slow down and pay attention to them today. Until suddenly something you totally never expected to happen, happens. They grow up and leave. And once they are gone, they may not have any more time for you than you had for them because they never learned from you how to slow down and enjoy each day. True enough, there will be a bunch more days. But there will never be another one exactly like this one. Check out today's unique sunset if you don't believe me.

72

(72) John's next photo is of a Carolina lily. He found this rare (for Mississippi) specimen in the swampy Pearl River County woods west of Picayune.

— John says: I always enjoy unusual sights or things to satisfy my amateur photography itch. Mr. Glen Ford of Picayune told me that he believed he had some Carolina lilies growing on a parcel of land, but he was unable to have that confirmed. He wanted some photos taken to find out for sure.

After I had taken the photos, I emailed one to the well-known horticulturist, Mr. Norman Winter. Very quickly, he confirmed that these were Carolina lilies.

— Walt: Isn't it nice that you never know what a day will bring, or a plot of ground? About the time you think you've seen or heard it all, something special comes along. And about the time you think nothing will ever change, it does. Today is not tomorrow. So I guess we should never stop expecting the unexpected.

(73) John's next picture he calls "Morning Song." This is a sunrise over Chester Lee Lake in northeast Hancock County.

— John says: It isn't good to begin a day harried and hurried, and Hancock County was still in the throes of hurricane recovery this week in June 2006. While enduring this necessity, it became my habit to seek any measure of spiritual refreshing that I could find. As I left my home that morning, there was an unusual tint to the predawn sky, a hazy, lemony flavor. I sensed an unusual opportunity and on my way to work, turned aside to the lake, one of my favorite places.

As the sun was just rising over the horizon and I walked to the shoreline, there were no sounds. No crickets were chirping, no birds welcoming the day, not even any distant highway noises. In a few moments though, a slight breeze sighed through the treetops but did not reach down to ruffle the water's surface. As I took the images, the breeze swelled lightly, producing a soul-filling musical peace that completed the scene perfectly.

— Walt: Descriptions like that can only make you wish you had been there also, so you could have experienced the same thing. But of course, if you had been along (or I had) it would not have been the same reflective moment.

73

74

75

(74) The next photo was sent in by Jonathan Robinson of Columbus, Mississippi. This is the Lowndes County Courthouse and Confederate Monument.

— Jonathan says: I was drawn to photograph the Confederate Memorial in front of the Courthouse for two reasons. The first reason has to do with the complicated and often painful history of our state. The second reason has to do with the eerie quality of light reflected on the monument.

— Walt: Our Confederate heritage is complicated. I know it is hard for some people to understand that we can respect the history of our state without sanctioning it. Personally, it is hard for me to ignore the Confederacy when I had a great-grandfather who was on the side of the South in the Siege of Vicksburg. And like the majority of other men serving in the Confederate Army, he was not a slave owner.

A family story attributed to Great-Granddaddy Welch says that at one point in the siege he and the other soldiers were issued their last rations: moldy bread. He threw it away because he considered it unfit to eat. A few weeks later, after folks in Vicksburg were reduced to foraging for roots and trying to boil their shoes for food, he went back to where he had thrown that bread and ate it.

(75) Jonathan Robinson submitted this next photo as well. It is the old rotating bridge in Columbus, Mississippi.

— And Jonathan says of it: The old river bridge in Columbus is a well-known and beloved landmark, especially in recent years. Columbus has established a beautiful River Walk Park along this section of the Tombigbee River, and the park has become a favorite spot for local photographers. I wanted to capture the beautiful sunset just as it touched the bridge.

— Walt: Old bridges are another of my favorite photographic subjects, right there alongside old barns and old churches, because bridges, too, have so much to do with life. Not often, but now and again, I think about how long it took for pioneers in their wagons, and for that matter, even farther back to Native Americans in their canoes, to cross a river that we can drive across in a matter of seconds on a modern bridge and think nothing of it.

The bridge should be an invention in the same category with the wheel because of its time- and labor-saving attributes. And old bridges especially. They perform their function while still retaining the character and flavor of the era in which they were built.

76

(76) Maegan Blair of Pinola sent the next photo. She calls it "An Unforgettable Wedding Day." The photo is of the Corinth Baptist Church in Magee, Mississippi.

— Maegan explains: This is a picture of my husband and I on our wedding day. Two days before our wedding, on my birthday, a tornado destroyed our church. As you can see, not much was left. We managed to pull everything together, with much help, and move our wedding to a different location. We thought it would be special if we went and had our picture made at the church on our wedding day. This picture is special to us because it shows that God is in control of everything. Jeremiah 29:11, "For I know the plans I have for you," declares the LORD, "plans to prosper you and not to harm you, plans to give you hope and a future." (NIV) God took control of our plans and made them how he saw fit.

— Walt: Just when you think you have God figured out, He tops Himself. Scientists thought they had everything all figured out when they rewound Einstein's universe and came up with the big bang theory. Now, they have redone the math and decided there is way too much gravity out there for way too little visible matter. So they've theorized dark matter to make up the difference. And even more recently, those equations have come up short, so they've had to plug in dark energy. And they have no clue what dark energy could be. What they have estimated is that according to the math, the universe that we can see with our eyes and with telescopes and detect with radiotelescopes and microwave receivers can be no more than about 4 percent of what has to be out there. So what we see is not nearly what we get with the universe.

So quit trying to hang your faith on being able to figure out God. We can't even figure out the part of the universe we *can* see, especially since scientists have proved that there has to be more to it than we know about. And if we can't even fathom what's before our eyes, how are we going to figure out the Author of it all?

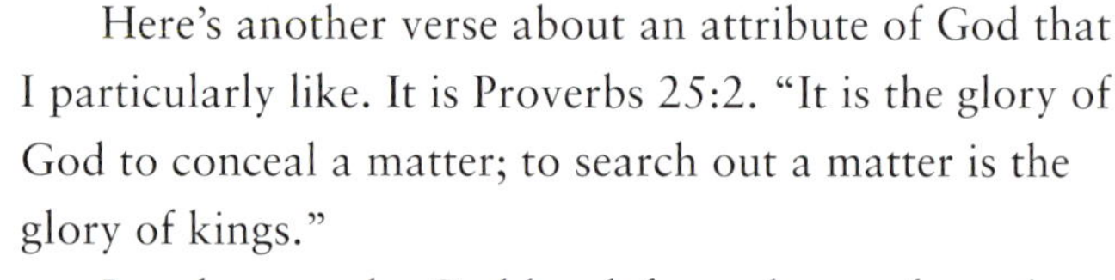
Here's another verse about an attribute of God that I particularly like. It is Proverbs 25:2. "It is the glory of God to conceal a matter; to search out a matter is the glory of kings."

77

In other words, God has left us plenty of puzzles to work on to keep us busy for a while into the future. And when we finally *do* figure out the secrets of the vastness of the universe, then we can start on the secrets of subatomic structures: structures which, by the way, can't exist in the same universe with all the big things according to the equations as we know them now. Yet obviously they do.

Go figure.

(77) Kay Alford of Greenwood has sent us a picture of her grandkids playing King of the Hill.

— Kay says: This is two of my grandchildren who live at Seven Pines in Carroll County. Their dad was making a road with red clay when they decided to play King of the Hill.

— Walt: Our games of "King on the Mountain" as we called it, were a lot more rough-and-tumble than what we seem to be seeing here. Of course, we were a bit older and were all boys and had a larger group. We would contrive and execute strategies to try to dislodge the king on top of the mountain that would make any general of any war proud. And when the king came tumbling down, all our alliances with each other to dethrone him would instantly dissolve, and we'd then become every man for himself to try to be the next king. Which usually just resulted in a pile of kids squirming around on top of a pile of dirt.

(78) Hank Lamb of Greenwood sent in this next photo. He calls it "Cotton Shack." It is in the Eden community in Yazoo County.

— Hank says: This house was on the south side of Eden. As you drove from Yazoo City it was on the left. Like so many others, it has been torn down.

— Walt: The only thing constant is that things are always constantly changing. Not only are the old tenant houses where the people who worked the cotton fields by hand disappearing, so are the cotton fields. You are hard pressed to find a cotton gin in Mississippi any more. It has all gone to corn and soybeans. Not that that's a bad thing. It's just different from years past when cotton fields were as white as a snowfall by the time October got here. And the sides of the road were frosted with cotton that had fallen off the trailers on their way to the gins.

78

(79) Hank Lamb also submitted this next photo. He calls it "Early Morning Courthouse."

— He says: Downtown Greenwood is punctuated by the Keesler Bridge and the LeFlore County Courthouse. Both are caught here as dawn's first light shines on them.

— Walt: Hank shows us the results of an applied lesson in photography. Time of day is as important an element in the finished photograph as the subject. At high noon, this scene would have made a rather bland picture. But in the warm glow of sunrise and in the way the low light models and sculpts the subjects with highlights and shadows, this picture is a great shot of downtown Greenwood.

79

Some of my friend Stephen Kirkpatrick's most striking nature photographs are of subjects still drenched in morning dew. Try this sometime if you want to take a nice photograph. Have your camera set up by the time the sun comes up and snap a series of shots of whatever you are taking a picture of as the light grows and shadows shrink. Somewhere in there will be a photo you will really prize. Then go back home and take a nap.

(80) Another photo from Hank Lamb shows us a Delta sunset just south of Sunnyside. He calls it "Delta Reflections."

— Hank: Sunnyside is in the middle of the Eutah Bend of the Tallahatchie River a few miles south of Minter City in LeFlore County. In other words, it is smack dab in the heart of the Delta.

— Walt: People have tried to explain and interpret and reduce the Delta to some simple common denominator for a long time. Attempting to do that reminds me of the scientists and physicists and mathematicians trying to come up with one equation that explains how the whole universe works; only the universe is not nearly as complicated as the Delta.

But no matter the politics or the poverty or affluence or whatever, all parties involved can settle on a few agreed-on aspects about the Delta. And one of those aspects is how amazingly beautiful it can be in spite of itself. This photo is your proof.

(81) Here is another of Hank Lamb's offerings. He calls it the "Three Amigos." He made the exposure at Tchula in Holmes County. Hank says this flower field was just before you climbed from the Delta into the hills south of Tchula.

I recall making a black and white picture of a sunflower a while back. The reason I chose black and white was, I was videotaping the flowers for a *Look Around Mississippi* story with my video camera. Although the video was in color, the camera's viewfinder only

80

showed black and white. And the black and white image in the viewfinder struck me as particularly interesting. So I pulled out my 35mm camera loaded with Kodak Tri-X pan film and snapped a shot.

I thought it was also interesting that my color video camera only allowed me to see my subject in black and white. And my black and white camera's viewfinder only allowed me to see the subject in color. So whichever camera I ended up shooting with, I had to use my imagination to picture the final result.

81

(82) This next shot is another from Hank Lamb. Hank calls it "Golden Bayou." Hank says each fall this bayou near downtown Tchula goes golden.

Back when I was a kid, coming home from Grandmother's house in Fulton going back to Greenville, we'd drive pass the swamps on Highway 82 just west of Greenwood. Usually the water was green with algae. I was telling my big brother David about how you could walk on that green stuff. He set me straight pretty quickly. And didn't let me forget it for a while, as big brothers will do. Same thing he did with me the time I made a comment about how airplanes could land on clouds. Professor Big Brother and Physics 101 corrected me again.

I made a decision right then to catch him in a mistake or in a lack of understanding about something sometime in his life and make fun of him forever about it. Wouldn't you know I'd get the only perfect brother in the world? I haven't caught him in anything yet.

But I'm still looking.

82

(83) Hank Lamb has a shot of the summer cotton crop just south of Cruger. He calls it simply "Summer Cotton."

I mentioned taking trips to and from Grandmother's house in Fulton from our home in Greenville. When you travel from the far edge of the Delta to the near edge of the

Appalachian foothills, you get to see a lot of varied real estate and varied agricultural applications. Back in those days, the fields were always planted in cotton, soybeans, or corn, unless you were passing a dairy farm, and then you might find wheat straw and alfalfa. And home gardens still lined the roadside too because the tenant farmers grew their own vegetables.

A good cotton year, as I recall, usually meant cotton stalks by July that were already over head high in the Delta. Cotton never seemed to grow that tall in the hills. A cotton field growing as pretty as the one in Hank's picture would elicit many favorable comments from the folks in our car as we passed by it.

83

(84) Frank Lay of Winona takes us into the hills a few miles from the Delta with his picture he calls "Carrollton Baptist Church at Night." He says the church was founded in 1833. This stately church sanctuary was dedicated the fifth Sunday of December 1895.

— Walt: Carrollton has some wonderful church buildings. I did a story on stained-glass windows in Methodist church buildings in the Delta several years ago. Clarris McDonald, the wife of the Methodist District Director, invited me to see the churches she and her husband had discovered while visiting and worshiping in all the churches in their charge. We went from Ruleville and Minter City all the way back to Carrollton. I recall the beautiful window in the Methodist Church in Carrollton had just been damaged by a hailstorm (it's since been repaired).

Carrollton still has some of the set dressing painted there when they made William Faulkner's novel *The Reivers* into a movie in the village back in the 1960s. Even today the quaint signs just fit right in with what you'd think a town of that vintage ought to look like.

84

(85) Frank Lay continues his church theme with "Rainbow Over Springfield Church Near Morton." Frank says the church is located just south of Morton out in Scott County.

— Frank says of it: The photographer saw this beautiful scene following a stormy day. He also served as pastor of Springfield Baptist Church for eight years.

— Walt: If you look closely, you'll see that it is a double rainbow. No sense in having a storm if it can't end in a rainbow.

85

(86) Britney Anne Majore sent in the next four photographs from her travels in various parts of the state. The young girl on the swing is in Cary in Sharkey County at the Cary Christian Community Center. Britney says when she was in high school, she traveled with a group of people from her church to help do renovations at the Community Center, found this young girl playing on the playground, and snapped a picture of her.

86

(87) Britney's next photograph was taken at Horn Island.

— Britney says: I have spent some of the most tranquil and marvelous moments of my life on the Barrier Islands of Mississippi. Summers growing up were spent here, graduations, high school parties, family trips, every special occasion happened on the islands! Although I've found connections to myself in many lands and countries, I still believe that there will always be a piece of my soul in the Mississippi Barrier Islands. Thoughts of swimming in the phosphorescence, first kisses, dancing in moonlight, and sliding down the fresh banks after a Gulf dredging will stay with me forever.

— Walt: Not to mention the sunsets.

87

(88) The next picture is of the Old Dowdville McMillan Store, Dowdville, Mississippi.

— Britney says: First, it took me forever to figure out how to spell the name of the Dowdville! We have passed this store every Sunday that we attended church at my dad's childhood church, Carolina Presbyterian, and my dad has always called it the "ole Dodville store." This was the first time I've had the chance to find the correct spelling. But I have always admired it and wanted to peer into the windows. So recently, we finally pulled over and did. There are not many of these old Mississippi store beauties left. I remember seeing so many of them growing up. I wanted to photograph this one before it is knocked down. I especially like to hear the stories behind all the old stores, like about all the farmers playing

ROYAL CROWN
COLA

88

WILLIAMS BROTHERS INC.
Est. 1907
Williams Brothers

89

dominoes, drinking coffee, and sharing the community gossip together in the old Madden store. I really used to like visiting the ones that had baby pigs and small animals for sale in the back.

— Walt: According to Jim Brieger's invaluable reference book, *Home Town Mississippi*, *Dowdville* is eleven miles southwest of Philadelphia. It's not too far from Madden just into Neshoba County to the east. Which puts it close to the one old-timey store in Mississippi that is still in operation, Williams Brothers Store just outside Philadelphia.

(89) This is a photo I snapped of Williams Brothers when I was there to do a *Mississippi Roads* story. I was talking to the current proprietor, Sid Williams, and he told me a few years ago his claim to fame was that he is Archie Manning's brother-in-law. Now he brags that he is Eli and Peyton's uncle!

(90) Next, Britney takes us to the Pascagoula River, to Creole Bayou.

— Britney says: This is my favorite bayou in the Pascagoula River. In the summer, if we were not in the Gulf, we were in the river for sure.

— Walt: The houseboat reminds me of a visit we made to Billy Joe Johnson's houseboat on the Pascagoula. He's tied up on the west side of the river near where the Highway 614 bridge crosses. Billy Joe loves God, and the river. He says when he gets up in the morning he has only one decision to make, to go up river or down river. Or if it's raining, he rolls over and goes back to sleep.

90

91

(91) Mandee Tatro sent in the next picture and calls it "Warm Depth." It was snapped just after a tornado at Olive Branch.

— Mandee says of it: I was impressed by the scene because the sky was the most amazing color considering what had just happened. The color of the sky lit up the tracks and pulled my eye through the depth of the tracks.

— Walt: This carries the silver lining around every cloud to the next level—gold. Some of the most violent storms I have ever experienced seemed to clear to a beautiful sunset after it was over. Husbands and wives almost like to get into an argument because after the storm they'll get to make up. Same principle.

(92) Nancy Jo Maples is our next photographer. Nancy Jo lives in Lucedale, Mississippi. The first of her two submissions is a photograph of the old Boler's Inn on Old Jackson Road in Union, Mississippi.

— She says of it: Boler's Inn was built by Wesley Boler in 1835. It was used as a stagecoach inn on the Jackson Road. During the Civil War, General William T. Sherman spent the night here in February 1864.

— Walt: I would suppose that an even more remarkable fact than Sherman's staying there would be the fact that he didn't burn it afterward! Ralph Gordon of Union invited Jo and me up for a tour of the area before I was to speak at the annual Chamber of Commerce banquet that evening, and Boler's Inn was one of the places we visited. Ralph has written a poem about the place and Sherman and all. We mused over why we thought the town was spared when Sherman saw to it there was nothing left of nearby places like the depot at Newton and the whole town of Meridian. Best theory Ralph has come up with is, it just couldn't set well if Sherman burned a place named Union, when it was The Union Sherman was supposed to be preserving.

'Course, that's assigning a higher scruple to Sherman than most Southern scholars are willing to allow him.

92

(93) Nancy Jo's next submission is entitled "Scratching Post." If you are in need of just such a utensil, the post is in Lucedale.

— Nancy Jo says: Plenty of famous folks have eased an itch at Bailey's Scratching Post in downtown Lucedale. Located on Mail Street, the original post was erected in 1939 as a promotional gimmick for the Bailey Insurance Agency. Visitors to Lucedale who have scratched here include Ernie Ford, Dizzy Dean, Ronald Reagan, and Tom Lester.

(94) Elmer Marmon of Columbus gives us our next photo. Elmer lists his age as eighty-four. He is a member of the Four County Electric Power Association. This is a photograph of the peppers for sale at the Farmer's Market in Columbus.

Elmer has quite an eye for composition and balance and color. To me, some of the best photographs are the subjects I would walk right past, like a display at a farmer's market, but that for some reason catch the eye of another photographer.

That's another rule for the serious photographer: Keep your eyes open all the time. Great shots can happen and then get away from you in just a few moments. There is an addendum to this rule about being aware of photo opportunities that present themselves:

93

94

Take out your camera and shoot them when you see them. Many "once in a lifetime photographs" are *just* that, once in a lifetime chances to catch a fleeting moment that won't ever happen that way again. Don't lose it by thinking you'll catch it next time it happens.

I keep thinking of eddies of swirling fog blowing across Pelahatchie Bay on the Barnett Reservoir like miniature tornadoes as sub-zero weather was howling in. In my defense, I was in a hurry to get somewhere else. But how absurd for me to actually think, "I'll get this shot next time the weather turns like this." I've been waiting for nearly thirty years. So far I've seen nothing approaching the foul conditions that one frigid day when I didn't have time to stop.

(95) Elmer captured this photograph for us, too. This is a panorama of the north side of Main Street in Columbus.

What an interesting shot of color and symmetry! The obvious can be so elusive when looking for a subject to photograph. I'm sure I've missed plenty of good shots when they were all around me if I had just taken the time to look closely at the composition hidden in the surrounding clutter and click the shutter.

Moving to the philosophical and making an application of that principle, life probably has a lot more wonderful elements to it than we realize because we haven't taken the time to crop out the clutter and focus on the pleasing compositions.

95

(96) Martha Powell of Brandon sent in the next photograph. This is the Red Bluff west of Columbia twenty minutes or so, to the north of Foxworth off Highway 587 near the community of Morgantown. Martha reminds us that Red Bluff is known as the "Small Grand Canyon of Mississippi."

— Martha says: Being raised in Columbia, I will always have a very special place in my heart for Red Bluff. As a young child, I remember the excitement of many Sunday afternoons spent there for family dinners (especially Easter egg hunts) and church outings. As a teenager, I had the thrill of following the trails to the Pearl River and climbing up the bluff. Because of years of erosion, the original road has been rerouted and you can no longer park at the edge. But it is still very easy to park and walk a short distance. If you haven't had the opportunity to see this amazing place, it is well worth the trip.

— Walt: I always add this disclaimer when doing anything pertaining to Red Bluff. It is private property! Even though there are no signs saying so, and even though there are trails in it and through it and up one side and down the other, it is not a public park.

96

The one time I hiked the trails at Red Bluff was the dead middle of summer. And as soon as we walked down below the lip of the hill, any hint that there might have been a cool breeze died.

Back in those days my camera came in two rather bulky pieces; the camera itself was hooked with an umbilical cord–like cable to the recorder, which was about twice as bulky as the camera.

We hiked across the railroad tracks to the Pearl River to the east of the bluff. There is a huge sandbar from where rainwater and spring water flow out of the eroded bluff, washing residue into the Pearl. We followed the stream back into the woods to the base of the bluff itself. We met many people hiking in there. One couple explained they were Mississippi potters and used only clay from Red Bluff in their creations.

Then we headed back to the trail for our climb out. When we reached the foot of the trail, it looked twice as long and twice as steep as it had when we came down it. I was already swimming in sweat, thinking about the hot climb ahead of us when it dawned on me that I *could* have done this story in January and not in July. Red Bluff would have still been there!

(97) Sonia McCardle of Brooklyn sent us this picture of apple bobbing. The photo was taken at Cypress Creek Missionary Baptist Church.

— Sonia says: You can still enjoy and experience the fun of a good old-timey apple-bobbing contest! This picture was taken at my church's fall festival. We had all the old favorite games such as apple bobbing, go fish, ring toss, and a cakewalk. Children and adults of all ages joined in on the fun and had a great time.

97

— Walt: I recall trying to bob for apples one time from my childhood. And that experience came at a church fall carnival, too. Either the apples were too big or my mouth was too small or the ice water wouldn't allow me to leave my face under long enough to get a grip. But I don't remember snagging any apples. Not with my teeth, anyway. I'm sure I scooped up a few with my hands.

(98) Here is another picture from Sonia McCardle of a place near Brooklyn, Black Creek.

— Sonia says: This picture was taken of a group of friends heading out on a float trip on Black Creek at Janice Landing in Perry County. Mississippi offers lots of fun outdoor activities to enjoy.

— Walt: I have been on Black Creek, and then farther south, on Red Creek, but never in a canoe. Both trips I was in a flat-bottom boat shooting stories. We zipped up Black Creek and beached on a sandbar and waded a cold, spring-fed stream a hundred or so yards into the woods to a little crystal-clear waterfall. A family had left a watermelon in the cold side stream at the edge of the big creek, cooling in the current while they explored the waterfall. As my guide and I left, they were all emerging from the woods and gathering back on the sandbar, cutting the watermelon and preparing to pitch tents and stay the night. By the time they were doing that, I was, of course, on my way back home to edit the story.

Sometimes I wonder what it's like not to be on a constant deadline and to have time to leisurely float down a stream? To *live* the story and not just shoot it? But then again, without deadlines and having to have stories, I doubt I would have ever seen Red Creek or Black Creek, even in a motorboat, much less a canoe.

99

(99) Here's another Sonia McCardle photo. She calls this picture "Beware!" It was taken in the Janice Community.

— Sonia says: This picture was taken of a copperhead snake found attempting to cross our driveway. After stopping for a quick photo session, my husband promptly made sure he was never to trespass in our yard again! After raising three boys in rural Mississippi, one of whom is fascinated with snakes, I've learned to appreciate the beauty in even poisonous snakes.

— Walt: Arrowhead hunting when I was a child at Grandmother's house in Fulton, I spotted this brown triangular shape up on a road bank in some leaves and thought I had found a champion arrowhead, until it blinked at me. Fortunately, I moved away very quickly. Any chance I would ever grow up to be an archeologist vanished that day. And there was never any danger of my becoming a herpetologist!

(100) Sonia McCardle gives us this next photo, too. This is a cotton field located in the Janice Community.

— Sonia says: Cotton can be used to describe the field or the sky in this photo. Cotton, peanut, and cornfields are abundant in south Mississippi.

— Walt: I'm so glad Sonia reminded me about peanut production in the state. Now I can add peanuts to my list of obscure plants and put it in rotation along with soybeans and

100 101

milo as answers to the question, "What's that growing in that field?" when I have no clue what it is.

(101) Mary R. Minor of Potts Camp sent in this photo of a coal chute in Potts Camp in Marshall County.

— Mary says: The coal chute was on the Frisco Railroad located in Potts Camp, Mississippi, and was destroyed in 1977 due to safety reasons, according to railroad personnel. It was a historical landmark and one that is missed very much by citizens of the town. I was editor of the *Marshall Messenger* (second weekly newspaper in Holly Springs) at the time it was torn down and wrote an article on the coal chute. I am also a resident of Potts Camp and am interested in historical buildings.

— Walt: I have had people tell me about an old building somewhere and go into great detail about it, and I get excited about going there to do a video story about it, only to have them go on to say it was torn down years ago. I try to tell them that it is difficult to make a story about where something *used* to be, when all that is there now is open ground or a subdivision or a shopping mall. (Although I have done it.)

Tearing down the coal chute for safety reasons reminds me of the old Observation Tower in the Vicksburg Military Park. It sort of looked like an open-air Leaning Tower of Pisa, only it didn't lean. There were several platforms all connected by a spiral staircase in the middle.

102

(102) This is an old postcard I picked up somewhere with a sketch of the Vicksburg Military Park Observation Tower.

I first saw the tower on an eighth-grade field trip from E. E. Bass Junior High in Greenville. Every year, Coach Dave Dunaway loaded up a few hundred eighth-graders in yellow school buses and hauled them to Vicksburg to discover history.

It was many years later before I made a trek back to the park on my own. And the main thing I wanted to see was the old Observation Tower. I searched the park over at least three times looking for it, only to find out later that it had been torn down years before for safety reasons.

I understand it took three bulldozers hooked to it with chains and pulling with all of their might all day long to get the "unstable" tower to ever fall.

(103) The next photo is titled "Low Tide" and comes to us from Tracy Pratt of Biloxi.

— Tracy says: We camped on Deer Island the evening before the Blessing of the Fleet 2009. I took this photo squatting down and

103

as close to the ground as I could. The low tide that day on the island made it so cool to explore all the treasures it had revealed.

(104) Tracy also submitted the next photo from Deer Island. She calls it "It's Alive! Crab."

— Tracy says: I love spending time on all the barrier islands. Deer Island of course is the closest and quickest to get to. We camped the night before the Blessing of the Fleet 2009 and as with any other time we camped on the islands, I like to grab my camera and stroll up the shore. There are always great photo ops. I thought this crab was dead when I snapped the photo. As I reached down to touch it, it suddenly scampered across the sand into the water. Scared the daylights out of me!

104

(105) Tracy closes her trio of island shots with this one she calls "Toes in the Sand." She's moved from Deer Island to Horn Island for this shot.

— And she says: We bought a boat at the beginning of summer 2009 after not having a reliable one to get us to the barrier islands for a few years. However, we missed the entire summer of 2009 at Horn Island because of boat troubles. In early November I was so happy to finally get to put my toes in the sand on my favorite barrier island.

— Walt: Somewhere in our house is a shoebox hand-labeled "Horn Island shells." I've managed to get out to Horn Island a few times. Not bad for not living on the coast and not owning a boat. But I find the barrier islands fascinating.

The sand that forms the islands washed there from rivers emptying into the Gulf of Mexico carrying away the tops of the Appalachians as the mountains weathered over the eons. And the islands aren't stagnant. They are ever moving westward. The islands get rearranged by hurricanes now and again. At the same time, they absorb some of the punch of hurricanes, thereby protecting the mainland somewhat.

Ocean Springs artist, potter, and eccentric Walter Anderson used to row the twelve miles from Ocean Springs out to Horn Island for extended stays of several weeks. (I point to that fact as validation of my observation that he was an eccentric.) His collection of watercolor renderings of the plant and animal life he painted while on the island were by and large unknown during his lifetime. After his death, his secret room was discovered at the Anderson family compound at Shearwater Pottery in Ocean Springs. And in it were thousands of his Horn Island paintings.

For a good feel for the barrier islands, read Anderson's *Horn Island Logs* and then visit the Walter Anderson museum in Ocean Springs. If nothing else, it will give you an appreciation for motorboats when you see the little skiff on display in which Anderson rowed out to sea.

106

(106) James H. Price of Dallas, Texas, sent the picture of the Mississippi River bridges at Vicksburg. Jim says he grew up in Noxapater and still takes care of his parents' home there. This is a shot of the river he took on a recent trip back home to Mississippi from Dallas. He is a member of the East Mississippi Electric Power Association and says he enjoys the *Today in Mississippi* newspaper.

What a great shot of sunset on the river. Of all the mighty and famous rivers on the planet, the Amazon, the Danube, the Nile, we have the Mississippi flowing right outside our back door. And just as people who live in Cairo, Egypt, drive past the Pyramids all the time and never give it a second thought, we drive past our awesome river and don't think much about it. But people in other parts of the world hold our river in just as much awe we hold in awe their enchanting landmarks.

(107 and 108) Bo Ray of Biloxi sent in a couple of photos of pelicans.

— Bo says of them: The shots of the pelicans were taken on the same day in Biloxi Bay. The pelicans were especially active this autumn. After the devastation of Hurricane Katrina, it was hard to imagine that the bay would ever be the same. But nature is resilient, and the pelicans are once again thriving and diving.

108

107

— Walt: Now that we have a few years between us and Katrina, I, too, am a little surprised at how quickly the coast has recovered to the extent that it has. Driving down Highway 90 just a few days after the storm I thought, like Bo, that it could never be the same. And in fact it isn't the same. In many respects it is better. And the scars that are still here will heal just like they did after Camille.

My daughter, Keri, pops up all the time encouraging me in the middle of a particularly difficult time, paraphrasing Nietzsche's saying, "That which doesn't kill you makes you stronger!" And Katrina didn't kill us. Even though we thought it might have for a while at the time.

(By the way, I appreciate the encouragement my daughter tries to give. But I remind her that there is always the outside chance that instead of making me stronger, the situation just *might* kill me!)

(109) Regina McIntire of Greenville submitted the photograph that she calls "Somewhere Over the Rainbow." She took the picture in Yazoo County. She says she always feels as if her own pot of gold is at the end of the rainbow somewhere.

I imagine there are still holes in the yard at 742 North Broadway in Greenville where we kids dug for gold at the end of many rainbows we created with spray from the garden hose. And there really is gold there! I recall a neighborhood boy lost a gold ring when it fell into one of those cracks that form in that Delta buckshot dirt while he was playing out in our side yard. We never found his ring, or any other gold for that matter. But we had fun in the water.

109

(110) The next photo comes from Reita Jackson. The old building is an old gristmill next to the Causeyville General Store near Meridian.

— Reita says: From what I could find out, the store and the mill were started in 1895 and are on the National Register of Historic Places. They house many of the original fixtures, a mechanical music collection, and some country and movie memorabilia. The mill is open for the public to view the grinding process every Saturday. And hoop cheese has also been sliced for customers for nearly one hundred years.

110

One of the very first feature stories I did at WLBT was at Causeyville Store. The script has long been lost. (Actually typewritten! *That* long ago.) I recall the proprietor of the store was a big movie buff and had been so enamored of the movies that he even went to Hollywood and worked behind the cameras for many years. He was a cameraman on Elvis' movie, *Blue Hawaii*. Then he came home to Meridian (Causeyville) and made the Causeyville Store into a mini museum, with an emphasis on movies. And the pound of cornmeal he ground fresh for me was especially tasty in the next batch of cornbread I made. (And yes, I make the cornbread. Ms. Jo's can't hold a candle to mine. She'll tell you.)

(111) Reverend Bruce Taylor in Decatur is our next photographer. He calls the photo of the old chair "Rocking No More." He took the picture in Decatur.

— Reverend Taylor says of it: The dilapidated rocking chair, hanging front door, and rotting porch are located at the Russell house four miles west of Decatur, Mississippi, where Union soldiers camped as they accompanied General William T. Sherman through Newton County on his Meridian Campaign. The photo reminds us of days gone by when time was spent in a rocking chair on the front porch visiting with travelers along the dusty roads, capturing a cool breeze as the summer sun was slowly engulfed by the horizon, or preparing freshly picked vegetables for cooking. The photo reminds us of simpler times now gone.

— Walt: In my *Looking Around Mississippi with Walt Grayson* book I told the story of meeting an elderly lady at the Pond Store in Wilkinson County who told me that when she was a child, on Saturdays her daddy would hitch up the team of horses and the family would ride into town, stopping to have coffee with all the neighbors on the way in, doing their shopping and visiting with all those same neighbors on the way out. And she said they had plenty of time to do whatever they had to do.

Nowadays, she said we have automatic dishwashers and clothes washers and clothes dryers and automatic coffee pots and microwaves and cars and don't have time for anything. What did we do with all the time we saved?

I have a couple of wonderful handmade Greg Harkins rocking chairs at my house. Most of the time they are decorations. The cats have time to sit in them. I seem to stay too busy. Maybe that's the origin of the term, being "off your rocker." When you don't have enough sense to stop and take time to sit and rock in them.

111

112

113

114

(112-113-114) Robert A. Pickett gets the award for living in a place I have never heard of, Kewanee, Mississippi. It's a stone's throw from the Alabama line east of Meridian on Highway 11-80. The photos are of his old family store and cotton gin.

— Robert says: These pictures are on behalf of my family's store, The Simpson-Wright Company in Kewanee, Mississippi.

The General Store was established in 1884, and along with the store there are an old cotton gin, gristmill, blacksmith shop, seed storage buildings, and outhouse. We are on the National Register of Historic Places, and you can find out a little bit more at our website: www.thesimmons-wrightcompany.com

The pictures are a front view of the store, the cotton gin, and the front of the store in the 1970s.

— Walt: I suppose we were a much more compact and self-sufficient society at the turn of the twentieth century. Here, the buildings in the village back then were about all you needed. Too bad things are always changing. Even before you can get used to what we have today, they are already morphing into what we will have to have tomorrow, and even then it doesn't stop.

I have said that I just wish they would quit inventing things, for at least just a little while, anyway. I'd like to feel as if I had a handle on something before it is outmoded by the latest thing.

I wonder how the old folks felt to see their complete and useful world at Kewanee start to slip out of style? I-20/I-59 bypassed the town. All the cars traveling through no longer stopped for gasoline and to buy a Coke like they did in the 1940s and 1950s. Cotton fell out of style as the main cash crop, rendering the gin useless. Supermarkets in town stocked a lot more items and sold them cheaper than could the old country store. Things faded to the point that we of the latest generation are left with a decision to maintain the facades of our old outmoded buildings, or just let them go and tear them down. And what of *our* kids who never *knew* the simple times in the old places that we once knew? Will they attach the same importance to the old places later in their lives that we do to the old places we know?

So I just wish they'd quit inventing things for a while and let us catch up and enjoy what we already have without having to make room for new gadgets while trying to figure out what to do with the old stuff.

(However, I am glad they came up with flat-screen TVs before I instituted my ban on inventions.)

115

(115) "The Colors of Spring" is what Sherry Roberson calls the next photo. Sherry lives in Scooba. This is a picture of Frances Roberson with her handcrafted quilts.

— Sherry says: Frances lives in Scooba, Mississippi. When Frances is not caring for her own large family, she is sitting with others or sewing on one of her handmade quilts.

— Walt: My Grandmother made a quilt for each of us grandkids. What a gift to make and give to someone! First of all, consider the time that went into each quilt. I'm sure at least a fleeting wish must have run through Grandmother's mind that her kids stop having kids! But maybe not. Symbolically, a quilt is a covering to protect you through the night, standing guard between you and the world when you are at your most vulnerable.

One of my prize possessions is the last quilt Grandmother was working on. She had finished the face before she passed away back in 1964. But just a year or so ago, my oldest aunt had someone attach the quilting and the back to that face, and then she gave it to me.

I have a little bit of an understanding of what it takes to make that quilt. So I appreciate this last of Grandmother's quilts more than I did that first "grandchild" quilt I was given back when I was about ten years old.

(116) The next photo was sent in by Robert Glenn Cliburn of Brookhaven. This is the Hartzog House in the New Hebron/Silver Creek community. Robert says he remembers this house from when he grew up there.

116

I suppose all of us have old houses from our childhoods that we remember. Some still stand; some only remain in our memories. Usually any time I dream about a house, it is the house I grew up in on North Broadway in Greenville. Everything our family did was centered around that house. Even if we went somewhere on a trip, it was always to that house we returned. I came home to that house from the hospital after I was born and didn't move away until I married. It seemed I lived there forever.

So I was surprised when Mama remarked one day, several years after Dad retired and she and Dad had moved back to Fulton to the house across the street from where she grew up, that she had lived in that house in Fulton longer than any other house she had ever lived in. It seemed to me that she had only been there for just a few years. I'm sure that it also surprised her to discover that the largest segment of her life came after Daddy retired.

The biggest chapter in all our lives could yet be out in front of us. That idea makes the day seem a little more important when you wake up every morning, realizing that something you do that day could turn the page to a whole new chapter in your life that you may not have even thought of before!

(117) Ronald H. DiPalma of Philadelphia submitted this old picture of his daughter and a friend that he calls "Dee Ann and William's Tomato Stand."

— Ronald tells us: My daughter Dee Ann, age six, and her neighborhood friend William Jordan, also six, had gathered tomatoes from William's father's garden, dragged out an old table, and set up store on the dirt road across from our house on Bounds Road (now North Hills Extension in Meridian). I don't think they sold any tomatoes, but the image of them doing so was too good a photo op to pass up.

117

— Walt: This picture reminds me of one of my entrepreneurial ventures when I was a kid. We had pecan trees in our yard. And every fall I'd pick up pecans and take them over to the co-op and sell them. But one year I wanted to see if I could make a little more than they paid at the co-op, so I bought some little paper bags from the grocery store across the street, sacked up one-pound bags of pecans, set up a stand on Broadway in front of our house, and sold them for twenty-five cents a pound. I guess I must have done okay, because I stayed out there with my stand all day. I remember a car

118

from up north somewhere stopped and the lady wondered how I could sell "*pe*-cans" (long *e*, short *a*) so cheap. I pointed to the trees and explained they grew right there.

The shade from those trees provided an outdoor room for family and church gatherings in the summer, a baseball field, then in turn a football field for the kids in the neighborhood, and an income of sorts for not only me, but also for the black boys who came around in November and wanted to pick up the pecans "on halves."

Pretty terrific contribution for just a couple of trees.

(118) Joanna Bajsa sent in the photo of the bathtubs. Joanna lives in Oxford. She says the tubs are on display at an establishment that buys and sells all sorts of vintage toilet appliances on the side of the road between Oxford and Batesville.

The way Joanna cropped the shot makes it seem as if it is an abstract composition. But then you look closely and see that it isn't. It's a bunch of very familiar items. But we are used to usually seeing only one bathtub at a time in our homes, not twenty. So to see all those tubs catches us off guard for a moment. Good eye to capture the surreal in the very real.

(119) Here's another shot Joanna took. She calls this "The Connection." This bridge is near Yazoo City.

Bert Case of WLBT is the biggest railroad fan I know of, except maybe Don Cain, who also works at WLBT behind the cameras. Don and Bert have impromptu railroad fests in the hall at the TV station all the time.

So when I have a vague reference to a set of train tracks or a locomotive or an old depot in one of my *Look Around Mississippi* stories, either Bert or Don (sometimes both) can give me details such as the date when the tracks were laid, what rail lines have owned them, what railroad they took the place of, whether they are active or not, or in danger of being abandoned, and on and on.

I think I can understand the appeal of railroads. Look at this picture. The converging tracks as they go away from you pull you in and invite you to leave yourself behind and come explore. And the bridge is a tunnel into a new and mystical place. Real railroads can actually transport you like that. If you have an itch to see what's around the next bend, a train is the way to go. If you can't really go, then you can pull onto a set of tracks in your imagination and uproot yourself from where you are to where you'd like to be, at least for a minute or two.

119

(120) Sam Andrews of Vicksburg sent this picture from his backyard, almost. This is in the Vicksburg National Military Park.

— Sam says of it: This photo is important to me because I had seen this demonstration done many times. But until I was actually a part of the crew I did not fully appreciate the men who fought in the Civil War.

— Walt: Probably none of us fully appreciates what the men of the Blue or the men of the Gray went through in that war. After the first few months of the war when there was no clear-cut victor, many people of *both* nations, the USA and the CSA, grew weary of the fighting—fighting that was to continue for years to come.

120

I was doing a story at the McRaven Tour Home in Vicksburg one Fourth of July weekend about Civil War reenactors who were camped in the side yard doing a living history demonstration. One of the soldiers told me of an experience he had the night before while on sentry duty. He said he was walking his post, back and forth, back and forth, when all of a sudden he heard a noise in the underbrush. He said the hair stood up on the back of his neck. And he said that for just an instant, a fleeting moment or two, he was really there.

(121) Sam also gives us this shot of the cannons in the snow in Vicksburg. This was taken at the Battery DeGolyer in the Vicksburg National Military Park.

— Sam says: This photo is significant to me because it shows how tranquil the battlefield is today, as opposed to how it was in 1863.

— Walt: I guess you could go even further and say the result of the War Between the States, to a great extent, is what *bought* the peace that we enjoy in our nation today. Had the South been successful and the US been split in half, neither of the resulting nations, the USA nor CSA, could have emerged as the world power that our united country became in the mid-twentieth century. But the combined talents and knowledge and

121

landmass of *all* of the United States made us what we are. We just had to settle some things along the way.

(122) Samantha Melancon submitted the next photograph. This is the park behind St. Mary's Basilica in downtown Natchez.

— Samantha says: The park is so beautifully decorated with its massive live oaks and fountain. The cannon is from Cuba.

— Walt: I'll tell you a little bit of what I've been told about the park. It was a cemetery at first. But the occupants were removed around 1820 or so and taken to the present Natchez City Cemetery a few miles farther north up the bluff on the Mississippi River.

I think there is an old photograph somewhere of Jefferson Davis standing in the park near the statue of the Confederate Soldier. The fountain was completely refurbished over the last few years and is in perfect working condition.

122

(123) Just out of the frame of Samantha's photograph is St. Mary's Basilica. The church is an architectural masterpiece from the 1840s. And the stained-glass windows make the building a place that you must pop in and see sometime when you are in Natchez.

(124) Samantha gives us this next photo, too. She calls it "Life in Black and White." This was taken on their farm in Lincoln County.

— Samantha says: I thought this shot of the 2008 snow was so unique because the picture appears as though it was taken in black and white. However, it was shot in full color. The snow blanketed the ground and made everything look perfect. It gives you the essence of stepping back in time, to a more simple time. I told my niece and nephew that it was as if God decided to put his colors away and paint in black and white that day.

123

124

— Walt: The world is a pretty place when simplified by a coat of fresh snow. No need for color to amplify anything. The snow hides the imperfections, and the uniform color lends a feeling of peace. And it could be now or a hundred years ago.

Then it melts.

(125) Samantha Melancon submitted this shot, too. Of the same place as in the snow picture before, it looks like. She calls it "Morning Fog."

— And says: I captured this one early morning as the fog was lifting into the trees. It created such a serene look that I felt it camera worthy. I felt God in the quietness of the moment. The corncrib is a staple when traveling down the roads of Mississippi, housing feed, old cottonseed, rusted farm equipment, and history of days gone by.

— Walt: Samantha seems to have her camera handy all the time. And that's not a bad idea, either. What's the deal about a picture saying a thousand words? Imagine trying to describe with words alone the scene in the photo of the fog and the trees and the old building catching the early sun just so and the vivid green of the grass. You might be able to do it. But odds are, you'd leave something out if you were relying on memory only. And even if you did describe it, you'd still have to go on and tell how such a scene helped you relate to God.

Instead, with one good picture, you don't have to say a thing. Plus, with the photo we are there, too. And all of us are also hushed by the fleeting splendor of the moment.

125

(126) Sandy Warren of Benton sends the photo of the crop duster entitled "Down and Out."

— Sandy says: A crop duster drops down from the sky and lets out the chemicals that will help eliminate the pests from a farmer's cotton crop. While crop dusters, a.k.a. ag pilots, still fly over crops, many farmers now use their own machines elevated on wheels, called a high boy. My husband and I enjoyed watching his brother fly over crops, including our own cotton, back when we row crop farmed.

— Walt: Because we grew up in the Delta, Jo and I tease each other saying we don't have to worry about the bugs getting our bodies after we're buried because we've breathed so much DDT sprayed from crop dusters in our lives. Well, crop dusters and the mosquito fog machine they used to run up and down the streets of Greenville at dusk dark during the summer.

How smells can carry us back to other places or other times was emphasized to me early one summer when I had to go to the ag supply house to pick up baling wire for my uncle's dairy farm, and the supply company was already getting in its stock of cotton defoliant. When I got a whiff of the defoliant, it immediately carried me three months into the future when school would reconvene in September and back to the classroom. Evidently, the drift of defoliant wafting through the autumn air was a smell I associated with where I was at the time I smelled it every year; back in school.

126

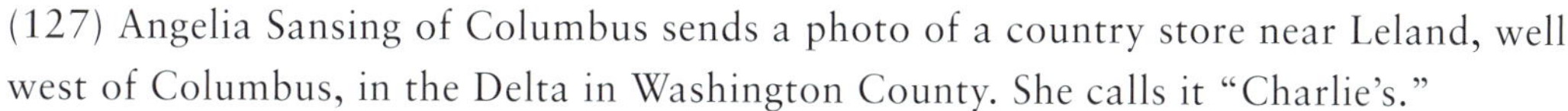

(127) Angelia Sansing of Columbus sends a photo of a country store near Leland, well west of Columbus, in the Delta in Washington County. She calls it "Charlie's."

— Angelia says: This is a picture of Charlie Fratesi's store we would walk to every day to get a bottled Coke. He always had pickled eggs and pigs' feet sitting on the counter along with penny candy. He also sold cold cuts, gas, and anything else you might need. He always had a few folks shooting the breeze, but I remember Shed Mister and Slim Tarpley.

— Walt: I don't want to start sounding like Daddy recalling the old days when he had to walk to school in the snow, but kids these days don't know what they are missing by not having a neighborhood store.

Usually the family that ran the store lived in a house attached to it. In my case in Greenville, the family who owned the neighborhood store across the street from us had kids my age. And any time any of us neighborhood boys went over to visit them after school, more likely than not we'd end up helping stock the drink box or something. But that led to one of the great advantages of having friends whose family ran a store. It was a cinch to come up with seven RC bottle caps for admission to the Thursday morning kiddy show at the Paramount Theatre. All you had to do was just be the one to empty the bottle cap collector off the drink box until you found enough.

127

128

(128) Cherry Sims of Mantachie sent in our second photo of the Beverly Drive-In in Hattiesburg. There is a black-and-white shot of this same subject earlier in the book.

— Cherry says of the Beverly: The Beverly Drive-In Theatre, a wonderful drive-in with a true Southern colonial flare, though long silent, still occupies a place just off Highway 49 on the south side of Hattiesburg. Many college students graced her presence as she offered the latest movies for their entertainment. My husband and I went to see A Charlie Brown Christmas at the Beverly for a honeymoon treat in 1970. We still tell folks about the Beverly and her role in our early married life. We made this photo of the lady on a visit to Hattiesburg for a college reunion in May 2008.

— Walt: Years ago I did a story about the Beverly Drive-In and the lady who lived under the screen. Sue Hargroder and her husband opened the Beverly in 1948. Sue stopped regular operations after his death in 1987. However, the screen was still in good shape and all the equipment operable in 1994 when I did the story.

In 1950 they built the Beverly's unique feature, their nine-room home including a sun porch, under the screen. No one thought it odd that the family who ran the theatre lived there. Drive-ins were new back then, and no one knew exactly what they were supposed to look like. And why the name Beverly? Sue told me it was simply a name she had always liked.

The Beverly could have been resurrected before Hurricane Katrina. But the storm pretty much brought down the curtain on the Beverly.

(129) Barbara A. DeBlasi of Gulfport submitted this shot of the lighthouse on Ship Island. She calls it, "Lighthouse Under the Moon."

— She says: This photo of the lighthouse on Ship Island was taken in August 2005 right before Hurricane Katrina took it out. Notice the moon just above and to the left of the lighthouse. One of my most enjoyable excursions is a trip to Ship Island with family to enjoy the sun, fun, and water. But sometimes a quiet stroll along the island brings just the peace and tranquility one seeks. This scene is a fond memory of the island before Katrina wreaked her havoc with our land and our lives.

— Walt: The lighthouses on Ship Island have had an interesting career. When Jefferson Davis was the United States secretary of war, he proposed the first lighthouse on Ship Island, as well as the fortifications, for protection of the Mississippi Gulf Coast. Ironically, it was retreating Confederate forces abandoning the island in the Civil War who set fire to that first lighthouse so the Union couldn't use it.

Skipping forward after a few replacements were built, a group of teenage campers sometime in the 1970s let a campfire get out of control and burned down what remained of one of the replacement lighthouses. It was that wooden lighthouse that was reconstructed on the island around 2000. Then (before I ever had a chance to do a story about the new/ old lighthouse) Katrina came along. And as Katrina was the end of the story for the latest Ship Island Lighthouse, I'm glad Barbara got a picture of it for us.

129

(130) Taylor Dean of Columbus sent in a photo of a bald cypress slough near Columbus.

— Taylor says simply: This is a very pretty slough off a dirt road containing bald cypress.

— Walt: Mr. Bubba, the congenial black man who was host at Tallahatchie Flats B&B (rescued tenant houses from the Mississippi Delta, collected and redecorated as places for tourists to spend the night. Money Road, Greenwood) once told me that he had always thought the only thing that lasted forever was the Word of God. But after working with the materials in the old Delta houses, he added, "The Word of God and cypress."

Mississippi cypress trees are as old as the California redwoods, some of them (the ones that survived harvesting in the 1920s and 1930s). The world's largest bald cypress is a hollow tree in the Sky Lake swamp near Belzoni. Seven of us walked inside the hollow tree one day when the lake was dry from drought, and there was plenty of room for at least seven more people to come in and join us.

But superlatives aside, the real value of cypress is captured in Taylor's photograph, their stately beauty and tranquility and insulation from time for a few moments as you contemplate how long they've been there, in a cypress grove in a swamp, or a slough.

(131) Taylor Dean also submitted this next photo, "Boat by Columbus Lake."

— Taylor says: This is a small boat and a beautiful sunset on Columbus Lake.

(132) This is another Taylor Dean shot, "Beaver Pond in the Fall." Taylor was taken by the pretty colors at this beaver pond in the fall of 2009.

131

132

133

(133) Taylor also sent in the next shot. This is of the River Walk Bridge in Columbus.

Old churches, old houses, old bridges, old barns, and old cemeteries are among my most favorite photographic subjects. I suppose I am trying to capture old times. I have to remind myself that today will be the "good old days" at some point down the road, and therefore, try not to hurry past today without at least giving it a chance. But since we don't know what is ahead, living right now is stressful. Maybe that's why we like the old days. Because we know how they turned out.

(134) Taylor Dean gives us the photo of the old trucks, too. Taylor calls the picture "Old Truck Selective Color." These are some old trucks at Waters International, which has several locations in Mississippi, but this is in Columbus.

And Taylor reminds me of another category of old thing I like, old cars and old trucks. I own a couple of old trucks: a1957 Chevrolet pickup and a 1946 Ford pickup. And the 1946 is a movie star. They used it in *My Dog Skip*. I even drove it in a couple of the scenes where it appears. I was dressed in a derby hat, a coat and vest with dress shirt and tie and a pair of cut-off blue jeans shorts. There is no air conditioner in old trucks. You have to wear one.

I think the way Taylor Dean manipulates the color of his photographs is interesting. I need to find out what program does this and buy it for my computer. Enhancing the colors to amplify the major focus of the image makes the meaning of the picture just that much stronger.

(135) Taylor's next shot is of a "Tree in Silo" near Columbus. Taylor says it is an unusual silo with a tree growing inside.

Do you wonder if the tree goes all the way to the ground inside the silo? Or is it growing out of some ledge near the top? And if so, how does the ledge support all that

134

135

weight? And if not, the trunk of that tree must be really skinny to reach the ground. Wash the whole scene in yellow rays of a setting (or rising?) sun, and you have a picture that you can study for quite a while and not really know the answer to your questions. But some of life's best questions are just posed, and never really answered.

(136) Michael Daniel Tew sent in the next photo. He gave it no title.

— But Michael says of it: My grandmother is teaching me to feed our chickens. I loved her. She taught me how to pray circa 1942. Clark County, Mississippi.

— Walt: She taught him to pray. I wonder if grandmothers still do that with their grandchildren? Probably about as many as used to, I guess.

I've prayed a bunch of prayers in my life that were never answered to my satisfaction. Needless to say I was disappointed at that. But on the other hand, I've prayed other prayers and got *exactly* what I asked for, and afterwards, I was *really* disappointed! Someone once wisely said that more tears have been shed over *answered* prayers than unanswered.

The more mature you get in your prayer life, the more your prayers come into alignment with the things God has said in His Word that He wants for us. But it sure is nice if you had someone like Michael's grandmother to take the time and the effort to teach you to pray in the first place.

136

(137) Elmetra L. Patterson of Louisville gives us the picture of "The Watermelon Man."

— Elmetra says: I remember as a child how we would take a box of salt and go sit in the watermelon patch and eat watermelon. Mostly, we'd eat the heart out and throw the rest to the cows. This is definitely Mississippi for me. This is Eddie Littleton with a look on his face that says it all. "I can't believe it is this big and I can't believe that I can pick it up."

— Walt: You have never properly celebrated the Fourth of July until you have sliced a Smith County watermelon on the Fourth. (Although someone reminded me that some of the best Smith County melons are actually grown in Covington and Simpson Counties.)

Jo and I went to a Simpson County watermelon patch a few years back and did a story about raising, picking, and selling melons on the roadside. I remember the grower telling me with pride how it was to go through the patch tossing melons onto the trailer as he pulled them off the vines. He beamed with pride as he told me how every now and again he would pick up a melon so heavy that it buckled his knees when he tried to straighten up with it. He'd grin and tell himself, "I grew that!"

137

138

(138) Elmetra Patterson shares this next photo with us also. The title of the picture is, "70-year-old man with his toddlers—twin sons."

— Elmetra says: This photo is significant to me because it is of my father, "Papa," and his last children, out of twenty-two. He was seventy years old in this photo with his twin sons who were toddlers. He was a World War I veteran, a farmer, educator, and just a great man. He was born May 8, 1889, and died December 5, 1959. His father and mother were born as slaves and came to Mississippi in 1863 from Newberry, South Carolina. The twins are now fifty-one years old. They grew up not knowing their father as I did but have turned out to be outstanding young men. They are Clifford (left) and Clifton (right). Out of twenty-two children, they were the only ones with nicknames, Big Man and Little Man. Papa would not allow us to have nicknames. He served in the war near Normandy and Brittany, France.

— Walt: Mama was forty-one when my younger brother Robert was born. Daddy was forty-eight. Mama wanted to wear a bag over her head. Daddy wanted to wear a " hero" badge. But can you imagine being seventy and having twins? The phrase, "Just shoot me now," comes to mind. But obviously this was a loving and proud "Papa" in the photo.

I was fourth of five children in my family. My mama was twelfth of twelve (ten who lived to adulthood) in her family. Mama mentioned to me one time that if the "pill" had been developed a couple of generations earlier, there would have never been a "her." So you know where that would have put me!

(139) Elmetra Patterson sent in this next photo of her son, Reginald, playing violin in Haiti. If you recall the January 2010 earthquake in Haiti, then the significance of this photo is even more apparent.

— Elmetra says: This photo is significant to me because it is of my son, Reginald Patterson, who loved to come to Mississippi from Milwaukee or California and hang out with the cows and the chickens at the barn when a child. He is presently an instructor and Ph.D. student at Duke University. Actually, he is a miracle because he had just left

Haiti an hour before the earthquake (January 12, 2010) rocked Port Au Prince. He was in the air when it happened. He played violin while in Haiti and taught improvisation to a music class. He has a degree in music performance from Oberlin Conservatory and a degree in French from Oberlin College. He moved to Louisville, Mississippi, with his parents in May 2006 and loves the quiet country life in Mississippi when on school breaks.

139

(140) Valerie Harris originally submitted this next photo to the "Picture This" section of the *Today in Mississippi* newspaper published by the Electric Power Associations of Mississippi back in 2007. Valerie lives in Anguilla. The photograph is of the *American Queen* coming underneath the new Mississippi River Bridge at Greenville.

I got to walk across the bridge a couple of years ago. I marveled that they could build and pave a bridge before constructing the connecting roads that lead up to it on either

140

142

shore. And that's quite a shot to get the riverboat going under it. The old and the new.

(141) Peggy Woodard sent in the next three photos. The first is of Pleasant Hill Baptist Church on Rockport New Hebron Road in New Hebron. Peggy calls it "The Light of the Sun."

(142) The next is a shot of sundogs; the rainbow effect created by the setting sun's rays being refracted by ice crystals in high cirrus clouds. Peggy calls this photo "Circle Rainbow," and she took it on Crooked Creek Road at Silver Creek.

(143) Peggy's last photograph is titled simply, "Rainbow." She took it on Ferguson Mill Road

in Monticello. This is an unusual rainbow because it is so low to the ground. Most rainbows have a high arc. The reason for this one's low altitude is the time of day. It is still rather early in the afternoon. The higher the sun is in the sky, the lower the rainbow. The really tall rainbows usually happen right at sunset.

It's interesting that all of Peggy's pictures are dependent on sunlight; the glowing windows of the setting sun pouring through the church, the sundogs, and the low-flying rainbow, and yet the sun itself isn't directly in any of them. It's the action of the sun on something else that creates the subject. Or rather, how something else reacts to the sun's light shining on or through it.

I suppose there could be a sermon whipped up from such examples. I'll try not to make it too sappy, but put it simply that sometimes we are the most appealing when it's not we ourselves that we are putting out front. But rather it is when we let the Son shine through us.

And unfortunately, that happens in a lot of us no more often than does a beautiful rainbow or sundog happen in nature.

143

(144) Jean Sharp of Lake submitted the next shot of the two boys and the fish. She calls it "Team Work."

— Of the picture Jean says: Our grandsons, Darren Watkins and David Watkins, shared the triumph of the catch in our family pond because David held the pole and Darren jumped in and grabbed the fish.

— Walt: I am trying to remember if my older brother Dave and I ever cooperated on anything like Darrell and David did in catching this fish. I'm sure we did. But neither of us have a trophy fish on the wall to prove it. Our sisters, Linda and Ermie, cooperated all the time. Well, from my vantage point it seemed they did. Both of them have beautiful voices and managed to put aside any squabbles they might have had to sing at church and at weddings and funerals and even on the radio in Greenville way back when.

But I more recall my brother and I fought a good bit while we were growing up. Mainly because I wanted to tag along with him and his friends, and he didn't want a little brother five years younger than himself hanging around while they were doing big kid stuff.

But it has been nice having an older brother lead the way all these years. For instance most recently when I was on the coast doing a seminar for the Mississippi Nursery and Landscape Association, Dave and his wife Rachael came over to Biloxi from Gulfport and we had lunch together. Now, I was approaching my sixty-first birthday at the time, and

Dave was about to hit sixty six. And as anybody over sixty can tell you, you don't look forward to birthdays after that point like you did when you were younger. Because along with any presents you might or might not get, you also get another year older. And that puts you yet another year farther away from youth and all that is involved in that that our culture seems to cherish.

But when Dave remarked that he had just gotten his first Social Security check, my day brightened. Heck, my whole *life* brightened! I almost hugged him for giving me something to look forward to again.

So brothers come in handy. Sometimes to help haul in a champion fish, other times to lead the way ahead and let you know the path is clear when you yourself can't seem to see the way.

146

145

(145) Alyce Catchot of Biloxi not only photographed the beautiful iris in her picture, she also raised it.

Something I have to remind myself of is, if I want pretty flowers in the yard the next spring, I have to plan enough ahead to plant the bulbs the preceding fall. That kind of simple discipline is tougher than you'd think for a fellow who usually doesn't think any further than two weeks ahead, much less two seasons.

But as I told my seminars at the garden shows this year, although we are the instant gratification generation, I have yet to see a yard and garden place with a drive-up window where you pull up and place your order for what you want your yard to look like on one side of the building and then drive around to the other side and they load up the finished project fully grown. Yards, like anything else worthwhile in life, take planning and then execution.

(146) Here is another of Alyce's flowers. This is a camellia.

— Alyce says of it: I photographed my camellias when they bloomed in November. Bees were feeding on them, and I captured their meal.

(147) Alyce moves from the garden down to the beach for her next photo. She calls it "Feathered Friends."

— She says: Here are a pelican and gulls roosting on some pilings at the beach. The color variations are interesting, as are the subjects.

— Walt: Birds of a *feather* may flock together, but evidently birds of ANY feather will rest together.

(148) Ann Armentrow of Florence submitted the picture she calls "Big Gator."

147

— Ann gives us the history behind this photo: When the Ross Barnett Reservoir was being built, there was concern about alligators in the Reservoir. My daddy, who grew up in Ridgeland in the twenties and thirties and spent any spare time he had on the Pearl River swimming and fishing, scoffed at officials who said there was nothing to worry about. He said there had always been alligators in the Pearl, and that the Reservoir would give them more space to live. This picture was taken in the 1930s of an alligator taken from the Pearl River by Ross Raymond and Johnny Reep, both of Ridgeland.

— Walt: The closest I have ever come to seeing someone levitate was when watching a news story about some Game and Fish people catching a gator near the populated area of the Ross Barnett Reservoir in order to transport him up the Pearl River north of Highway 43 and release him in the swamps up there. Bert Case was the reporter. It was night. They had the gator in the boat with Bert and a couple of the Game and Fish officers, when the gator made a big wiggle and broke loose from his captors' hold. The three people in the boat seemed to jump about three feet into the air and just hang there with their feet wiggling beneath them cartoon-like while the gator thrashed back and forth below them.

Earnest Herndon is a reporter with the *McComb Enterprise-Journal* and likes to take extended treks on the rivers and creeks of Mississippi. Several years ago I was following Earnest and two of his friends as they canoed the entire length of the Pascagoula River system including its two main tributaries, the Leaf and the Chickasawhay. We had

148

arranged a rendezvous a few days into their trip where the Leaf and Chickasawhay flow together and form the Pascagoula at Merrill to do an update to the story.

Earnest was telling me about the wildlife he had seen on the lower Leaf River (swallowtail kites, lots of deer), and described a particularly unnerving experience that had happened only a few miles upriver when Earnest was paddling close to the bank and surprised an alligator. The gator promptly shifted himself into high gear and splashed into the river and disappeared under Earnest's canoe. Earnest said he was a bit concerned because he wondered if the gator was just getting away or was about to do like the crocodiles in the Tarzan movies and turn and snap the canoe in two.

The boats in these stories remind me of another instance involving a snake instead of an alligator. Both are just as dangerous to me because I'll hurt myself trying to get away from either. This fellow was fishing in the willows of an oxbow lake in the Delta when a water moccasin fell off a willow limb and dropped into his boat. In a knee-jerk reflex, the man grabbed his pistol and shot the snake several times. And sank his boat.

(149) The picture of the RC drink machine comes from Ben Atkinson of Philadelphia.

— Ben says: This is an old RC Cola cooler from a Scooba antique store. RCs and Moon Pies used to be a treat for kids in Scooba.

— Walt: As well as elsewhere. Slipping into my "I remember the good old days" mode, I remember coming home from grade school and getting a quarter from Granddaddy Grayson, taking it across the street to Bertschler's Store in Greenville,

149

buying a Coke and a bag of potato chips and having fifteen cents left over. My three-second-theory of economics theorizes that our present global financial instability all started when soft drinks went up to six cents from a nickel.

Let me say a word about my three-second expert opinions about things. These are my theories about such disciplines as geology—specifically how the world was formed—and anthropology and archeology and so forth that experts in the field will listen to as I articulate them, and actually consider them for about three seconds before they dismiss them out of hand and turn to go on about their work.

The first time I proffered one of my theories was in the DeSoto National Forest while doing a story about an archeological dig into what turned out to be an Indian mound at Camp Shelby south of Hattiesburg. The archeologist in charge was excited and very pleased with himself that they had proved this rounded pile of earth had, in fact, been made by man. They proved this by digging into the middle of the top of it all the way to the base some eight or nine feet down and finding artifacts. A natural mound would not have had artifacts that deep.

This was a significant find because this was a part of the state in which no mounds had been discovered previously. But that wasn't the *big* news. The artifact they had dug up at the base level of the mound was a Clovis point! Clovis projectile points (a fancy name for a spear point) are named for the area of New Mexico where they were first discovered and have been dated to about fifteen thousand years ago. If this was a Clovis point and it was that old, then that would almost double the accepted amount of time people had been in this area, previously believed to be eight thousand and certainly no more than ten thousnd years.

As the professional archeologists were reveling in their discovery and taking off their hats and fanning themselves and grinning and laughing, I simply said, "You know, Camp Shelby is a National Guard training facility, and troops from all over the country come here. What if some Guardsman from New Mexico had picked up this point back home, and while he was here training it fell out of his pocket?"

The two archaeologists looked at me with a puzzled look on their faces for about three seconds, and then they turned and went back to their merrymaking.

Now, I'll grant that my theory might have been a little off track. But on the other hand, have you seen any scientific papers published proposing the moving of the timeline for human habitation of the lower Mississippi Valley back several thousand years? So I'll let you be the judge of the validity of my theory.

(If at this point it takes you much longer than three seconds to decide to turn the page, then you are thinking way too hard.)

(150) Charlotte Harris of Escatawpa gives us the old photo of the classroom.

— Charlotte says: Second grader Annie Martin and classmates at Bayou Casotte school about 1925; a glimpse into education's past.

— Walt: I'm wondering if it's close to Christmas in this photo. There's a table display

150

with what looks like a house, a tree, and a reindeer. Plus most of the kids have their coats on. Mama was about the age of these kids, and we have photos of her with the same Buster Brown haircut that a couple of the girls have.

I started off this book talking about the box of old pictures that I would entertain myself with by looking through on rainy days. One thing that stands out about old photographs is their ability to freeze the moment. And frankly some of the clothes and haircuts frozen by them end up being way out of style.

For instance, when we were in high school a Beatle shag "cut" was modern and hip, even on the boys.

One day not too long ago Jo had pulled out one of our high school annuals from Greenville High from back in the late 1960s to look up someone and had left it lying out on a table. So our granddaughter Taylor came over and picked it up and tried to find Jo's and my pictures in it. When she found us, I never should have asked Taylor what she thought. I figured she would comment on how young we were or how handsome I was. Instead, she just giggled and said all of us looked goofy. I was highly insulted until I took a step back and looked with new eyes. And truth is, we too were a little out of style.

However, I am also of the age to know that I don't have to get upset over her saying something like that. Because from my advanced perspective, I know someday Taylor will have a grandchild looking at her high school picture and giggling at nose rings and boys looking like a lawn mower ran over their heads.

'Course, by that time, that same child will look at *my* picture from *my* high school days and see it in the same light I see the old oval portraits of my great-grandparents hanging on my oldest aunt's walls—or Mama as a beautiful child with a Buster Brown haircut.

What's new turns old, and then turns out-of-date, and then turns charming. And what's new that follows us to replace our newness will grow old some day, too, all at the speed of time, the speed of life.

(151) Speaking of old times, Dean Meador Smith of Hattiesburg sent in this modern photo of an old log cabin.

— Dean says: This is an1885 log cabin as it looks today restored. My great-grandfather was a Methodist circuit rider. He married many couples on these front steps since this was on the main road from Hattiesburg to the Rawls Springs Community.

— Walt: My first reaction when I see a shot like this and hear the story with it is a longing to go back and live in those "good old days" that were so simple and uncomplicated. But of course, those days were anything but simple. If you wanted meat for Sunday dinner (lunch) you had better have slaughtered and preserved it last fall or gone hunting earlier that week. Vegetables came from the pantry and were canned in a hot kitchen way back in the heat of summer last August when the garden came in, after you planted it, hoed it, watered it, picked it and then hulled/peeled whatever it was you harvested, then cooked it, poured it up into jars, and stored it. All of this was in addition to all the other things that had to be done at the same time, all without electricity or running

151

152

water or a way to travel any faster than your fastest horse.

Have you ever wondered, if the people of those "good old" days were given a choice of living in their labor-intensive days or our days of automatic everything and pushbuttons and fast food, which would *they* choose?

(152) Here's another old photo. This one is from James B. Herrin of Clarksdale.

— James says: The details of this photograph were told me by my mother Minnie L. Brown Herrin, whose father was Thomas Jefferson Brown, Sr. (known as Tom Brown). Tom Brown was a farmer, businessman, and county supervisor who lived in Holmes County, three miles west of Ebenezer on the Ebenezer-Coxburg Road.

My mother knew the names of all but four of the men in this picture. My grandfather was grading roads in Yazoo County about 1913 in the area of Bentonia, Wade, Desenville, and Vaughn Station driving a team of oxen.

— Walt: Can you imagine grading a road with oxen? That isn't anything I'd consider as being a part of the "good" in the "the good old days."

(153) Jean Sharp in Lake sent the shot of the roosters.

— Jean says: These Japanese black-tailed buff roosters (hatched spring 2009) seem to be enjoying the early morning peace and quiet.

— Walt: On North Broadway just inside the city limits of Greenville where I grew up, I could hear roosters crowing from houses a block or so away. Now I live in the country, and I can hear school kids playing at recess from a nearby grade school, but I never hear roosters. Times change.

153

(154) Jean Sharp of Lake also sent this photo. It is of her paternal grandmother, Allie Hawkins Harrison. Jean titled the photo "Spinning Wheel" and says the spinning wheel is still in the family.

In my Grandmother Cummings's house in Fulton were many treasures: arrowheads; old newspaper clippings; ancient telephones; books over a hundred years old; an old radio that, even though it didn't work, we still weren't allowed to push its buttons; and a spinning wheel. As a child, I never could fathom how on earth you could make thread with the thing, as we were told was its original purpose. But for us kids we pretended it was the steering wheel on a pirate ship or a part of some mechanical device that either generated electricity or chopped people's heads off, depending on which set of cousins was in on the game.

Several years ago I was doing a story about the Pioneer Pilgrimage that they used to have in Monticello and they had a spinning wheel demonstration just like the one in the picture, which was just like the one at Grandmother's house. It was set up and in use and making thread from wool. Once you see it operating, it makes perfect sense how to use it to turn cotton or wool into thread. (Sort of like a computer nowadays. Once you see the grandkids use it, it's obvious how it works.)

154

My sister Ermie has the spinning wheel now. And its primary function today is to knit all of us in the family to our past, which it does very well, even though we rarely ever get to see it anymore, now that it is tucked safely away in North Carolina.

By the way, you may be interested to find out how, out of all the plethora of aunts, uncles, cousins (and a few steps thrown in for good measure) in our family did my sister manage to be the one to scarf up the spinning wheel? Simple. She was the first one who *asked* for it! Never occurred to any of the rest of us to just up and ask for it. Makes me wonder what *else* I missed out on in life by keeping quiet. I suppose

155

I could go check out my sister's house and find out! Ermie points out that Mama got the spinning wheel the same way—by asking her own mother for it, many years ago. And that a new generation of grandchildren have all played our same old games with it.

(155) Jean Sharp of Lake also gives us the picture of the giant pumpkins.

— Jean says: My daddy, Larther Harrison, (1910–2000) ordered five big pumpkin seeds and planted them and grew these three nice pumpkins in his garden sometime back in the 1980s. This is his grandson, Nic Harrison.

— Walt: I was intrigued last fall when a lady who had an ornamental banana tree in her front yard in west Jackson called me and said it had sprouted bananas. She was flabbergasted that bananas would grow and ripen in Mississippi. After that story aired, I got a call and was invited to Magee to see a fruit salad growing in another back yard, oranges, lemons, bananas, and pineapples. I asked the grower why he went to all the trouble to try to raise tropical fruit like that in un-tropical Mississippi. He replied, "Just to prove I could do it."

I imagine we all take on a project now and again for the same reason. That may be why we have this picture of giant pumpkins.

(156) Kathy Stump of Olive Branch dug up this old photo of "Baptizing in the Delta" from the 1940s.

— Kathy says: This photo is very precious to me. My father is getting ready to

156

be baptized. The location is in a blue hole at Waxsaw, which is between Rosedale and Gunnison. I'm not sure the date, but we think it is the early 1940s. The church is Gunnison Baptist Church.

— Walt: Kathy goes on to say that Clarence Lawson is her father, and he is the sixth candidate for baptism from the left.

An old preacher remarked to me one time that the reason all the revivals were held in the summer in the old days was it was too cold to baptize in the winter. There was more to it than that, of course. The lull in growing crops came around the end of July and the first of August when the corn had already been "laid by" and the cotton wasn't ready to be picked yet. That gave a great window of opportunity to hold a protracted meeting. But I also bet the temperature of the baptismal water in summer as opposed to winter probably did play a part in setting the date for holding meetings designed to get folks saved.

In my days as a college student preacher at my little country church, I remember hectic summer nights during our revival meetings. My "evangelist" one year was a fellow student at Mississippi College. And one night we got such a late start for little Good Hope Church some seventy-five miles from Clinton that we had to run eighty and ninety miles an hour all the way to get there on time. I worried what a poor testimony it would be if we got a ticket. Then I decided not to confess if we did. And we didn't. Don't remember if anyone was saved, but at least we weren't lost.

157

(157) Mary and Phil Cliburn of Mendenhall sent us a shot of the home they designed and built themselves and then got snowed on. At last it is snowing again in Mississippi (as of 2008, 2009, and early 2010) and everybody has a chance to get the obligatory photos of their houses in the snow. I wonder if folks in Minnesota take pictures of their house every time it snows?

(158) Speaking of snow, Stacy Beard of Collins caught this cardinal during the January 2008 snowfall. Stacy says she loves the stark contrast between the red bird and the white snow.

The only time I lived outside Mississippi was back in the winter of 1970–1971 when I moved to Omaha pursuing a career in major market radio. I figured I'd get to see a white Christmas in Omaha, but no. Our first snowfall came on New Year's Eve of that year. And I didn't see the ground again until well into spring. As soon as the snow melted enough to safely get a U-Haul on the road in the spring, I came back home to Mississippi.

My newsman on the 6:00 until midnight shift at KOIL radio was Kirk McMichael. Kirk gave me some sage advice as far as living in a snow-plagued climate like Nebraska. He told me to tie a snow shovel upright to the front bumper of my car and start driving south. And when I got far enough that someone asked me, "What's that thing tied to your car?" I had gone far enough. Move there.

158

I remember the first color in an otherwise bleak winter in Omaha came one March day when I looked over the snow bank blocking our exit out our back door and saw a redbird in a bush in the backyard. I had hope again.

(159) Here's another picture Stacy Beard sent. She calls it "Sunset on Little Black." The photo was taken in Purvis.

— Stacy says: Sunsets in Mississippi are some of the most beautiful of anywhere I've ever lived. I never get tired of them, and this one on Little Black Creek in Purvis is one of my favorites.

(160) Wilma Holland offers a photo of her two great-nephews wading in a creek beneath an old iron bridge near their home in Meadville. Wilma says wading in a creek is one of her favorite childhood memories.

Maybe Wilma has hit the nail on the head. In Mississippi, we still enjoy sharing favorite memories of things we loved to do in childhood, not only with each other but also from generation to generation. Things like wading in the creek as she did as a child and now her great-nephews are doing. Or flying a kite off the levee along the Mississippi River, or walking barefooted in the sand (or mud), or watching the stars blink on at night and trying to make a wish on the first one, or picking out the winter constellations, or catching lightnin' bugs in the summer.

Life really does fly by at the speed of time. But even though time is linear (so we'll never be able to build a time machine that carries us back or ahead in time) time also runs in circles, too. Snow in the winter, dogwood and wisteria in the spring, watermelon and lawn mowing in the summer, and turning leaves and sitting by fireplaces and reflecting on all of it in the autumn. Reflecting on the past and also planning for the holidays to come. Then the circle starts again.

159

We wanted to capture a great variety of Mississippi in this book. So that's why we asked all of you to send in pictures to be included. But it is also the circle of time that has been captured; school pictures, garden pictures, coming-of-age pictures, sunrises and sunsets. And the linear progress of time is also shown; young folks who are now old, old places that used to be new, places that are no longer here except in our memories and our hearts and photographs, time as a circle and a straight line at the same time.

A little far afield and maybe only another of my three-second theories again, but since the theorists who are trying to account for the big universe of stars and galaxies and the subatomic universe of quarks and what all can't seem to get a unified theory, and since they equate space as time; maybe they need to know time comes in two packets: circular, the seasons; and linear, bringing the ends of things after they've gone in their appointed number of circles.

160

But then again, it may be like the B.C. comic strip I recall of two of the characters gazing into the night sky and one reflectively remarking, "It sure makes you think, doesn't it?" And the other fellow, after a silent panel or two of more night gazing answers, "About what?"

I think that life is like my theories. If you have to take much more than three seconds analyzing it, you missed the point.

(161–168) I asked a friend of mine, Nathan Culpepper of Meridian, to let me select some of his photos to include in this book. Nathan has a keen sense of composition and juxtaposition and irony that he presents like visual poetry in his photos. These next shots are Nathan's. I use his descriptions of each photo.

(161) "Thanksgiving at the Farm."

This image is special to me on a personal level. If for some reason I had to keep only one of my photos, this would be the one I kept. This little house is located on some land that belongs to my family. That land is where I spent nearly every holiday of my life—including Thanksgiving until the year 2003. You see, my family had this little tradition. We would all meet down there for every Fourth of July, Memorial Day, Labor Day, and Thanksgiving. It wasn't the most fancy place to meet, but the little house would be busting at the seams with aunts, uncles, cousins, grandparents, etc. Everyone would bring a little

161

food, and we would just spend the day on the porch talking and visiting with each other.

This place belonged to my grandfather, and he loved nothing more than to have the entire family down here for these events. He was always the last to eat, making sure that everyone else had everything they needed before he would stop for himself. My grandfather passed away in 2003, and our holiday tradition died along with him. We tried to continue having it down there, but it just wasn't the same. We closed up the little house and forgot about it.

Time (and a couple of hurricanes) have had their way with our little camp house for seven years now. Most of the roof is gone and the floor is rotting out inside. The ceiling is falling in, and it won't be there much longer. My dad lives just up the road from here on a different part of our land. We were out there on that Thanksgiving as we searched for a new tradition, and we visited the little house on the day that used to have such a different meaning than it does now. Just as we pulled up, the sky opened up and was shining down on this special place. Maybe it was coincidence, or maybe it was something else; either way, it was a nice reminder of the times we used to have there, and I wasn't going to let it go by without taking a picture to remember it.

162

(162) "Center Pivot."

The center pivot in action is a common sight in the Mississippi Delta during the summer. These

163

marvelous contraptions keep our crops growing healthy, no matter what the weather decides to do. I love this photo because it sheds a whole new light on this workhorse of the farming industry. To people in the Delta, center pivots are so commonplace that no one gives them a second thought. As a temporary transplant to the Delta, I was fascinated by center pivots and the work they do. My photography career has been relatively short. I started seriously taking pictures in early 2006. This photo was one of the first that I was truly proud to call one of my works. I had the idea in my head for months before the opportunity to take the shot presented itself, and I am more than happy with the results that I got. It is my hope that this photo can help bring attention to how much beauty there is in Mississippi, and especially in the Delta region.

(163) "Thank You."

This photo is my way of saying "Thank You" to all the veterans out there for what they do for us. The Doughboy monument in downtown Meridian was built in honor of the World War I veterans. The flame on top is lit every year on Veteran's Day and left to burn all night. It means a great deal to me to be able to create images like this. We would not be the nation we are today without the sacrifices of our veterans. We should all say "Thank You" every chance we get.

(164) "Lamb-Fish Bridge."

There are not a lot of drawbridges in Mississippi, but Lamb-Fish Bridge is one of them. This bridge was built to accommodate river traffic on the Tallahatchie River that carried goods to and from the giant Lamb-Fish Lumber Company at Charleston in the early 1900s. The vertical lift section of the bridge is no longer in operation, but the great superstructure of the bridge is still intact and is a wonderful thing to see. When I look at this photo, I

164

can just imagine what it was like around 1920 to have to stop on a rural dirt road in the Mississippi Delta to watch the road raise up in front of you and let a boat pass by on its way to the mill. This bridge doesn't have a lot of years left. The superstructure has been rated poor, and the bridge is considered to be structurally deficient overall. I am happy that I was able to visit this place and preserve it for history with this and other photographs that I have of it.

(165) "Muddy Mississippi Road."

This photo was taken while I was on a last-minute commissioned shoot for a client. I was given a deadline of one week to shoot, edit, and print photos of a family farm for my client to give as Christmas presents. I was more than pleased with how this one turned out. In trying to capture the memories of the family farm, I inadvertently got a photograph that is so typical of what many Mississippians see in the rural areas of our state every day. What says "Mississippi" more than a red mud road, pond, and barn? The shoot was a complete success, the client was more than happy, and I will always have this picture to remind me of what Mississippi is all about.

(166) "Sea of Grain."

I like this picture because it epitomizes what the Mississippi Delta is to me. It seems like every day that I am there, the day ends with a beautiful sunset over an expanse of land that stretches to the horizon. We should all be so lucky as to have that view every day. I

165

hope others who cannot visit the area can appreciate the beauty of the area through my photographs of it.

(167) "Threefoot Sunset."

To me, this picture represents Meridian. I was born and raised in Meridian and have passed by this building my entire life. It has been abandoned for many years and hasn't been in the front of many people's minds (including mine). This all changed recently when the building fell into disrepair and was threatened. The previous mayor of Meridian went on a campaign to save the Threefoot Building and was successful in making a deal with HRI, the same company that just renovated the King Edward Hotel in Jackson. The plans were made to transform this old office building into a state of the art downtown hotel with convention center that would support our newly renovated MSU-Riley Center. Some citizens were overjoyed by this while others cried foul because of the money involved in the project. Now a new mayor is in office, and the future

166

of the Threefoot Building is again in jeopardy. The deal with HRI was nullified, and work to stabilize the facade of the building was halted. Now our Threefoot Building sits in limbo once again due to politics. If a deal to save this building is not reached soon, I'm afraid Mother Nature is going to make the decision for us and force this building to disappear forever.

No matter what happens to this building, this is the way I would like to remember it. I will always have this photo to remind me of how proud the Threefoot stands tall over the Meridian skyline and looks down on everyone here.

(168) "Twin Bridges."

This photograph is more about the aesthetics and practice of photography than the subject matter to me. Natchez is one of my favorite places in the state, but this photo doesn't really represent Natchez. Natchez is about history—antebellum houses and Spanish moss. This bridge is modern, with jagged lines and angles, and that's one of the things I love about this picture. The symmetry of the two bridges and the depth of the photo stand out. It also represents another form of photography that I don't practice a lot, and that's

167

long exposure. This photo was obviously taken at night, but the long exposure gives a color to the bridge and sky that is impossible to see, and it happened to turn out exactly as I hoped. The camera deserves all the praise for this one. It did all the work. I was just pushing the buttons.

168

Mis

Afterword

Well, that's the end of our collection of photographs. I sort of feel like we've been playing a game of Go Fish and have been asking everyone to "Show us all your Mississippis."

Obviously there is way more to the state than we have shown. But here is a sample of what the state means to some of us. It is old times and home places and families and beauty and proud people. And obviously, more than just a few of us are photographers, too. And our pictures are like flash cards that remind us of the things we feel are important, and thereby remind us of who we are.

Keep the cameras handy and try not to pass up any good shots. Don't misplace them. Show them off to friends and family when they come visit. In doing so, they'll come away with a whole lot better idea of who we really are as a people and what we really are as a state. And don't be surprised if someone going through your collection of photographs looks up and says, "Oh. That picture reminds me of . . . ," and then you are off on another storytelling adventure.

About the Author

Jo and Walt Grayson

Walt Grayson is a sixth-generation Mississippian, born and raised in Greenville. Walt came to Jackson in the broadcasting field in 1969 and has lived in the Jackson area since then with one notable brief exception he mentions in this book.

Since 1984, Walt has been doing feature reports for WLBT TV in Jackson. In 1999 he took over hosting duties for Mississippi Public Television's *Mississippi Roads* series.

Walt and his wife Jo travel the roads of Mississippi probably as much if not more than anyone in search of unusual people and places as well as historic spots and places of natural beauty to feature on television.

Some of the stories Walt has gleaned from the people of Mississippi as well as his own experiences make up much of what you will read in this book.